Exploring
the
Little Rivers
of
New Jersey

James and Margaret Cawley

Exploring the Little Rivers of New Jersey

Revised by the Little Rivers Club

Rutgers University Press
New Brunswick, New Jersey

Maps by Dick Anderson

Photographic Credits:

James and Margaret Cawley: Pictures on pages 9, 11, 12, 13, 15, 16, 36, 44, 47, 50, 59, 60, 64, 66, 71, 84, 87, 99, 113, 120, 132, 135, 136, 140, 142, 143 (bottom), 158, 161, 162, 169, 171, 173, 188, 196, 209, 211, 218, 225, 228, 233, 260

Margaret E. Cawley and Nancy Cawley Jerome supplied pictures from their family's collection on pages 254, 256, 258

Dick Anderson: Pictures on pages xiv, 7, 8, 10, 21, 24, 27 (bottom), 31, 40, 92 (top), 93, 94, 95, 96, 106, 128, 129, 131, 133, 168, 183, 184, 185, 191, 203, 204, 215, 216, 223, 269

Don Clopp: Pages 111, 112

Jim Ewin: Pages 69, 70, 72, 73, 74, 75, 76, 77, 166, 170, 172, 205, 206, 207

Ken Garrison: Pages 114 (top), 144 (top), 146

George Grant: Pages 14, 81, 82, 83

Al Hahn: Pages 32, 33, 37, 38, 39, 41

Al Hanna: Page 160

Don Irish: Pages 119, 121, 122, 123

Bryan Katz: Pages 150, 151, 153, 154

Christi Madsen: Page 230

Eric Madsen: Pages 43, 51, 55

Lloyd Ottesen: Pages 61, 62, 63, 65, 90, 91, 92 (bottom), 97

Jim Powers: Pages 189, 190

Dave Roszel: Pages 22, 25, 26, 27 (top), 197, 198, 231

Sid Shelton: Pages 103, 104, 107

Herb Slade: Pages 157, 159, 220, 221, 222

John Smith: Pages ii, 19, 20, 23, 42, 53, 54, 114, 115, 143 (top), 144 (bottom), 145, 177, 178, 179, 180, 186, 195, 199, 229, 232

Peggy Smith: Page 237

Bill Whitten: Pages 48, 49, 56

Fourth edition, copyright © 1993 by Rutgers, The State University
Manufactured in the United States of America

Library of Congress Cataloging-in-Publication Data

Cawley, James S.
    Exploring the little rivers of New Jersey / James and Margaret
Cawley.—4th ed. / revised by the Little Rivers Club.
        p.   cm.
    Includes bibliographical references and index.
    ISBN 0-8135-2013-4 (cloth)—ISBN 0-8135-2014-2 (pbk.)
    1. Rivers—New Jersey.   2. New Jersey—Description and Travel.
I. Cawley, Margaret.   II. Little Rivers Club.   III. Title.
F140.C3   1993
917.49'09692—dc20   93-1113
                                                              CIP

*Affectionately dedicated to our children
and grandchildren,
and future generations of canoeists
on the little rivers of New Jersey*

Contents

Preface

For centuries, canoeing was an important means of transportation for the tribes that inhabited what would come to be called New Jersey—it was as integral a part of their way of life as the rivers and streams that flow through this land. In part because of the ease of transportation, their settlements and villages sprang up along these waterways and flourished for many generations. Over more recent centuries, new settlements flowered as lumber mills, mines, forges, charcoal mounds, paper mills, glass factories, canals, and railroads arose in turn, peaked in importance, and faded back into near oblivion.

In this book the Cawleys reunite the canoe with remaining traces of early "Jerseyana"—using the canoe as a means of exploring our little rivers and searching out the spirit of the original inhabitants and later settlers amid the relics of an almost forgotten past. The canoe's skin of birch bark has long been replaced by aluminum, fiberglass, Kevlar, and plastic; its role as a means of transportation has given way to a new but equally vital purpose—offering a means of escape from the pressures of today's world. The feeling of going nowhere in a mad rush dissipates, stroke by stroke of the paddle. The peaceful feeling of canoeing may be even more appreciated today, as we launch this fourth edition of *Exploring the Little Rivers of New Jersey*, than it was when the Cawleys published the first edition in 1942. Yet during the five decades that bridge these two editions, many of the rivers have remained untouched by the burgeoning population of our rapidly growing state.

Like those who built the Indian villages, the forges, and the canals, James and Margaret Cawley are now gone; but they too have left many gifts for us to treasure. This book is one of those gifts. It is not only a canoeing book or a history book but rather a combination of the two. For decades it has motivated people to appreciate simple pleasures and to seek out the history and artifacts of those who have come before us in this land.

In a desire to extend this work to yet another generation of paddlers, a number of enthusiastic canoeists have come together to update the Cawleys' work. This ad hoc group of some two dozen individuals, now known as the Little Rivers Club, comprises members of the Murray Hill Canoe Club, the Bellcore Outing Club, and the Monoco Canoe Club, along with several additional people. All share a common love of canoeing and an ardent interest in preserving the Cawleys' book.

In updating the book a conscious attempt was made to preserve as much of the original work as possible. Small groups volunteered to reexplore various rivers to check the accuracy of the text and maps, making only the corrections necessary to update them. Since many of the original photographs were dated, teams volunteered or were assigned to retake as many scenes from the third edition as was practical and to take additional pictures where it seemed appropriate. Previously published pictures of historical significance were collected in collage form as a tribute to the Cawleys. You'll find these in the chapter "About the Authors."

Other changes we have made are the addition of Cedar Creek and the expansion of the Pequest River section. Both of these little rivers have become quite popular as canoeing streams over the years. Also, we have redrawn all the maps to show more clearly the roads and landmarks that today frame the rivers. In doing so we have taken some license with the scale, so we suggest that the reader consult county and topographical maps for further details. Finally, we have expanded the section "About the Authors" and changed the title of the chapter "Camping" to "Planning a Trip."

We who have had the pleasure and the honor of participating in this project wish to dedicate our efforts to James and Margaret Cawley, whom we never met but with whom we share a strong kinship of mind and soul. To extend this connection, we hope that some group of kindred spirits who have come to know this book through this fourth edition will assemble in a decade or two and carry on this work into the twenty-first century.

We wish to acknowledge the following members of the Little Rivers Club for their many hours of work in exploring, writing, editing, photographing, and all the other things that accompany such an effort:

Dick Anderson	Al Hood	Patrick Regan
Tom Busteed	Don Irish	Dave Roszel
Jim Ewin	Bryan Katz	Sid Shelton
Dave Fischer	Carol Maclennan	Herb Slade
Ken Garrison	Doris Maynard	John Smith
George Grant	Lloyd Ottesen	Peggy Smith
Al Hahn	Jim Powers	Bill Whitten

Special thanks to Dick Anderson for his many hours of labor in drawing all the maps for this edition. Thanks also to the many other individuals who have supported this effort over the past two years. Their names are too numerous to mention. And many thanks to Karen Reeds, who helped to make it all happen.

Finally, we would like to express our appreciation for the encouragement, insight, and assistance we have received from Margaret E. Cawley, Jeanne Cawley Marshall, and Nancy Cawley Jerome, with whom the authors "enjoyed many happy days on the waterways of New Jersey."

Exploring
the
Little Rivers
of
New Jersey

Exploring the
Little Waterways

Anyone familiar with the wilderness areas of the canoe country in northern Minnesota or Canada might believe this photograph was taken in such a place. It would be a natural assumption, but actually the scene is the Batsto River in the New Jersey Pine Barrens, where beautiful skylines of white cedar are commonplace. Throughout the Wharton State Forest and other areas of the Barrens are several rivers with equally entrancing views. As one quietly glides down the usually fast-moving, amber cedar water, it doesn't seem possible that one can return to the metropolitan centers within an hour by car. The New Jersey Turnpike and the Garden State Parkway carry the country's busiest traffic on the edges of the unique and mysterious land of the Pine Barrens.

One may explore the charming countryside of New Jersey by car or, better still, by quietly paddling a canoe down any one of the many little rivers of the state. Exploring by canoe enables one not only to savor the smell of the pines and cedars and observe the wildlife along the streams but also to get to know the rivers in a way not otherwise possible. Robert Louis Stevenson expressed it this way:

> There is no music like a little river's. It plays the same tune (and that's the favourite) over and over again, and yet does not weary of it like men fiddlers. It takes the mind out-of-doors; and, though we should be grateful for good houses, there is, after all, no house like God's out-of-doors.

NEW JERSEY

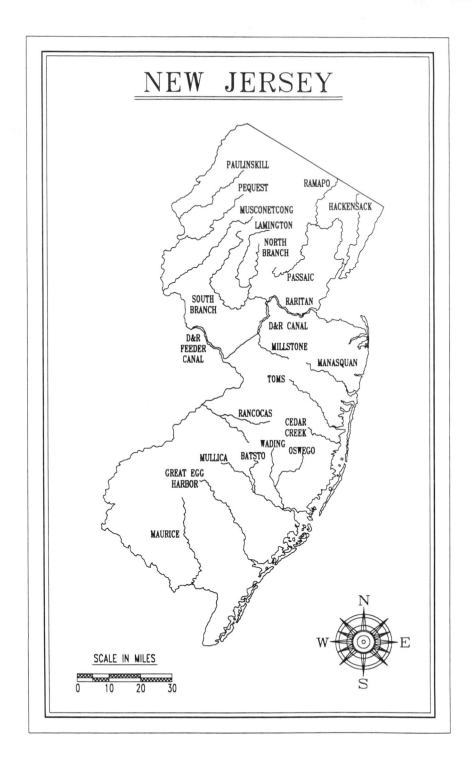

PAULINSKILL

RAMAPO

PEQUEST

HACKENSACK

MUSCONETCONG

LAMINGTON

NORTH
BRANCH

PASSAIC

SOUTH
BRANCH

RARITAN

D&R CANAL

D&R
FEEDER
CANAL

MILLSTONE

MANASQUAN

TOMS

RANCOCAS

CEDAR
CREEK

WADING

MULLICA   BATSTO   OSWEGO

GREAT EGG
HARBOR

MAURICE

SCALE IN MILES

0   10   20   30

N

W   E

S

And, we may add, a little river helps one to cultivate a sense of inner quietude so needed today. To be able to launch a canoe on a river where conditions are sometimes truly wild, where mile after mile stately white cedars surround the canoeist with beauty, where fast, foam-flecked water rushes around every bend, can make a day of rare adventure. In the Pine Barrens, which constitute more than one-quarter of the area of the state, remnants of forgotten towns from the early days of the Iron Empire can be found. As recently as a few decades ago, if one knew where to look, it was not difficult to find an operating still in some of the more remote places in the Barrens. It was the land of the smuggler and the privateer during the American Revolution, and even during the first half of the twentieth century, law enforcement officers found it better not to venture too far into some of these remote areas.

Not all the rivers are this wild, of course; yet even those in more settled country, like the Millstone, or the North or South branches of the Raritan, have a charm of their own. The quiet countryside, the cattle peacefully grazing in the meadows beside the streams, and the well-kept farms provide a different but equally rewarding experience.

The novice canoeist should not first attempt to navigate the wilder rivers in South Jersey. Begin by renting a canoe for a few hours' practice on such waters as the Delaware and Raritan Canal or on the canal feeder, where there are no snags to turn the canoe over. As for learning to handle a paddle, the Boy Scout merit badge pamphlet and canoeing publications by the American Red Cross are among the best guides we know. In addition, basic canoeing courses are offered regularly by the Red Cross, county park systems, and several New Jersey canoe clubs. For those who may be inspired by this book to try a real cruise, we have provided a chapter on trip planning.

Little problems such as carrying around a dam or over a fallen tree, getting wet from capsizing a canoe or from a sudden shower, and running aground on a sandbar or a stump are to be expected, and once you get accustomed to them are easily accepted as part of the adventure.

As the chapters of this book demonstrate, the rivers of New Jersey are rich with history. From the earliest days of colonial settlement, communities and industry were drawn to the rivers for power, transportation, and resources. We find evidence that long before then the Indians also enjoyed the benefits that a river can bring. Rivers carved out valleys that followed a gradual grade back into the hills. The gradual grade provided routing for the network of railroads that have left their mark throughout the state. Like the rivers themselves, many railroads have been abandoned by commerce, but their traces may be found in library books and in the roadbeds, bridges, and tunnels left behind.

A surprising variety of wildlife may be seen along New Jersey's little waterways. In some places, such as the Pine Barrens, many species of plant life will be found that are seldom seen anywhere else. You may wish to carry along bird and wildflower guide books; they will enhance your enjoyment of New Jersey's little rivers.

The Batsto

The origin of the name Batsto is said to be from a Swedish word meaning "place to bathe." When the Lenape lived along the shores of this quiet-flowing stream, they must have loved the solitude of the vast wilderness, crossed only by their footpaths and the game trails. Today that same forest area, now a part of the Wharton State Forest, is almost as wild, with none but the sometimes impassable sand roads providing access to most of it.

That we have the privilege of enjoying this wilderness and its rivers by canoe, as the Indians did centuries ago, is due to the foresight of the state legislature in purchasing the area and creating the Wharton State Forest in 1954. The 110,000 acres, approximately 165 square miles and constituting about 2 percent of the total land area of the state, is a priceless heritage, but the belief, held by many, that it will be preserved in its present wild state forever may turn out to be an illusion. Vested interests may one day succeed in obtaining concessions that will eventually destroy the wilderness of the Wharton Tract as they have destroyed other wild areas of the country.

Today as one paddles or drifts in a canoe from Hampton Furnace the only evidence of civilization encountered on the fourteen-mile journey is the railroad bridge a mile or two below the put-in, the campsite and the timbers of the former bridge at Lower Forge, and Quaker Bridge. The river is quiet and peaceful, and the hushed loveliness of sky, water, and woods offers a good tonic for the tensions of the modern world. We prescribe it in large doses for those so afflicted.

This stream is not one for casual afternoon paddling. It is truly

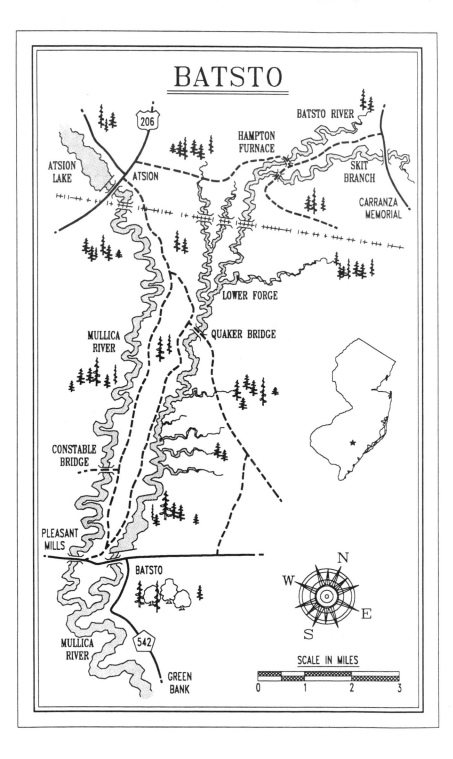

BATSTO

Rest stop on the Batsto, a place to lie back on the warming sand or contemplate the meanderings of a fallen leaf drifting on the water.

The now abandoned Jersey Central Railroad bridge that crosses the Batsto not far from the put-in at Hampton Furnace.

a wilderness river where, if anything happened to your canoe, the only way out is on foot over a sand road, if you can find one. We consider the Batsto and the Mullica to be the two least accessible rivers in New Jersey and therefore the most enjoyable for cruising.

As is the case with many of the Pine Barrens rivers, the source of the Batsto is difficult to find. Apparently, its beginning is a swamp pond north of the Carranza Road, three miles southeast of Tabernacle in Burlington County. It flows in a southerly direction through Hampton Furnace, Lower Forge, Quaker Bridge, and Batsto to the Mullica River, into which it empties a short distance below Pleasant Mills. While it is possible to begin a canoe journey at Lower Forge or Quaker Bridge, doing so is not recommended because of the poor condition of the roads. A better starting point is Hampton Furnace, a few miles above.

En route to a cruise on the Batsto, we had difficulty negotiat-

This view at Lower Forge is typical of the wild upper part of the Batsto.

| *Low bridge on the Batsto in early April.*

ing the water-filled holes on the sand road to our starting place. However, once we were afloat on this unbelievably beautiful river, with the blue sky overhead filled with cottony clouds, and with a perfect temperature for paddling, we soon forgot access difficulties.

After taking some photographs we swung out into the fast-moving current and were on our way to Quaker Bridge. We did not hurry and at times just drifted along with the current, thinking how fortunate we were to be able to enjoy such a beautiful day on the river. One of the greatest pleasures of paddling on a cedar water stream in the Pine Barrens on a warm summer day is the delightful odor of the white cedars that fills the air.

We soon arrived at Quaker Bridge and beached our canoe for a look around. We wanted particularly to find, if possible, the remains of the nineteenth-century Thompson's Tavern, which was a favorite stopping place for the patrons of the old Philadelphia-to-Tuckerton Stage Line that operated during the last century. We

The beginning of the sand road along the Batsto near Route 206. Sand roads such as this one honeycomb the entire Pine Barrens. At times they are deeply rutted and pockmarked with engulfing puddles.

failed to find even the foundation stones, nor did we see any other traces of the occupancy of the place.

Quaker Bridge might have been a large and important community had the plans for a railroad that was granted a charter in 1836 matured. However, the plans failed, so the hope for the future of Quaker Bridge died.

As we browsed around, we recalled the story of how the place received its name. It seems that Quakers from a wide area of the countryside used to walk overland to the place of their annual meeting. They had to cross the Batsto on the way, and there was no ford. People and horses had to swim, the horses carrying the old people and the children. Over the years several drownings occurred, and as a result, in 1772 the first bridge was built; it was logically named Quaker Bridge.

Along the shores of the Batsto from Quaker Bridge downstream many unusual wild plants like the golden spike, turkey-

The Richards mansion was the home of Colonel William Richards, the manager of the Batsto Iron Works. It is now a part of the restored historic village of Batsto and is open to the public.

beard, and fringeless orchid may be seen in season. Early in the nineteenth century the rare curly-grass fern was first discovered in the vicinity, a discovery that won international acclaim at the time. We tried, during our lunch stop, to find some of the rare plant but could not. Later on, through the courtesy of Miss Ann Carter of Batsto Village, we were shown a clump of the fern on the shore of a nearby bog. According to Miss Carter it is usually found under a white cedar tree near water and seldom grows to a height of more than two inches.

Having lunched, we shoved off again and soon encountered some heavy brush and small cedars blocking our passage. With our saw and hand axe we soon cleared the blockage. The sky remained clear, and the temperature rose a bit, making us somewhat sleepy from the soporific effects of the warm sun reflected from the water and the strong fragrance of cedar.

In midafternoon we arrived at the dam at the lower end of that part of the river known locally as Batsto Pond, where we left our canoe for a visit to the nearby historic Batsto Village restoration.

A bog-iron barge, well over 150 years old, has been excavated from the mud in a nearby stream and placed on view in the restored village. It was used to carry ore to the Batsto Furnace.

| *Iron ore from a nearby bog, on exhibit at the restoration at Batsto Village.*

Batsto Village was established as a bog-iron-producing operation in 1766 and during the height of its production was one of the most important of all such enterprises throughout the Barrens.

During the Revolutionary War, when the British tried to sail up the Mullica River to burn the Batsto Works, they encountered such resistance from the fleet of American privateers in the river at Chestnut Neck and from the Minutemen on the shore that they gave up the attempt, retreated to the ocean, and resumed their blockade of the lower river. As a result of the successful defense of this iron works in the Battle of Chestnut Neck, the Batsto Works continued to supply the American Army with cannonballs to the end of the war. Because of the British blockade of the Mullica River the ammunition was carried overland to Valley Forge and other points.

Abandoned for almost a century, the Batsto Works seemed destined for oblivion, but some years ago the Division of Parks and

Forestry began an extensive restoration, which is now completed. Thousands of people from all over the country annually visit this historic village, and it is well worth the time and effort for anyone interested in the days of the Iron Empire of the Pine Barrens. Several writers and historians have expressed the belief that restored Batsto Village is the nearest thing in New Jersey to Colonial Williamsburg in Virginia.

Returning to our canoe and making the carry around the high dam at the foot of the pond and over the low concrete dam below Highway 542, we resumed our journey. As we paddled around a bend, we saw a large stick beaver house on the right shore, and just below, another on the other bank. Nearby we saw an oak tree ten inches in diameter which the beavers had cut through and attempted to drop across the river. They had not succeeded, as the tree caught in the crotch of another tree on the way down. Two things were unusual about those beaver works: Beaver houses are usually built in water and not on land, and beavers do not, as a

Downstream about a half mile below Route 542 in Batsto, two unusually large beaver houses have been built on the shores of the river instead of in the water, as they frequently are.

An example of the cutting power of a beaver's teeth—this tree is ten inches in diameter. The work of the beaver that cut the tree down was useless, as in falling the tree was caught in the branches of another tree.

rule, work on hardwoods like oak—they prefer the softwoods like poplar.

After photographing the beaver works we continued to the mouth of the river and on downstream through the Mullica to the Mullica River Marina, where our car had been left.

Cedar Creek

A picturesque covered footbridge spanning a horseshoe dam makes the source of Cedar Creek well worth a visit. Surrounded by tall stands of cedars, Bamber Lake is one of the prettiest places in the Pine Barrens.

This area is rich in history as well, with the ruins of furnaces, forges, mills, and railroads revealing the extent of nineteenth-century industry along the banks of Cedar Creek. Ghost towns and cranberry bogs add touches of past and present to a river that has been home to Indians and settlers, forges and farms, beaver and heron.

The first quarter mile of Cedar Creek, from Bamber Lake to Lacey Road (Route 614) is difficult to explore from land or by canoe. It is really little more than a tangled mass of thorny brush and bramble with very little to recommend it. The only point of interest here is the few remaining pieces of an old Tuckerton railroad bridge located along the north side of Lacey Road. The railroad operated from 1871 to 1937 and ran from Tuckerton at the shore, through the small settlement of Bamber, to Whiting for connections with trains from New York City and Philadelphia. The rails and ties are gone now, but the abandoned bed is still easy to find.

As Cedar Creek continues its sixteen-mile journey from Lacey Road toward Barnegat Bay, the landscape is dominated by cedar and holly. The trees provide berries for the birds and a green canopy for the canoeist all year long. The section from Lacey Road to Dover Forge is generally canoeable, although it is easy to lose the

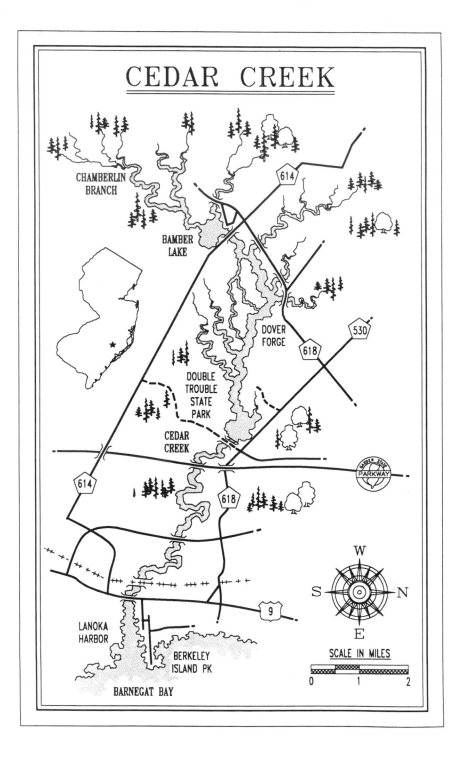

| *Birdwatchers at the Dover Forge access area.*

channel. The creek divides into many smaller streams through the swampy bogs, and getting lost is a distinct possibility.

A better place to start a canoe trip is the state access area at Dover Forge, two miles east of Bamber on Dover Road (Route 618). From this point the water moves along quite nicely as several small tributaries have added their flow to the stream. There are also many footpaths and picnic spots in the area, making this a good place to explore on foot.

Dover Forge was one of several forges and other business ventures owned by John Lacey, an officer who served under Washington during the Revolutionary War and later rose in rank to general. Lacey operated three forges and smelted bog-iron ore mined from the beds of Cedar Creek and other Pine Barrens rivers. He became very wealthy and influential, and today Lacey Township, a large section of Ocean County, is named for him.

Downstream from Dover Forge is an area where hundreds of trees have been damaged or felled by beaver. During a recent trip we found that several beaver lodges and a very large beaver dam had completely altered the character of the river. While we are

Cedar Creek as viewed from the parking area at Dover Forge.

usually pleased to witness wildlife doing well in New Jersey, the industrious beavers of Cedar Creek have flourished to the point of dominance.

Below this area is the stump-lined reservoir used for the reclaimed and reactivated cranberry bogs farther downstream at Double Trouble. The local cranberry operation is now only a shadow of its former self, but several bogs were restored to good condition in the 1970s and are still being worked. Double Trouble, now a state park, has many old buildings related to the early cranberry industry. There are also cottages, a one-room schoolhouse, a general store, and the old Double Trouble sawmill.

There are many accounts of how this area came to be called Double Trouble. The most widely accepted version, however, recalls that in the late eighteenth century the dam used to supply power to the sawmill was destroyed by a spring freshet. The mill owner had the dam rebuilt only to have it destroyed once again

What better way to celebrate the new year than on the river? Many groups participate in the annual January 1 canoe trip down Cedar Creek.

Beavers can drastically alter the landscape by taking down trees and building dams and lodges.

Beavers often provide unexpected challenges such as this three-foot-high dam below Dover Forge.

by another flood. He is said to have lamented that now he had double trouble, never imagining that he had given the sawmill and surrounding area a new name.

The bridge leading to the sawmill at Double Trouble is where most people begin their canoe trips on Cedar Creek. It is reached by following the main road in the park past the old sawmill and on to the river. Vehicles are permitted, but only to load or unload canoes. Be sure to park only at designated areas near the park entrance.

A few hours' pleasant paddling from Double Trouble brings one to the usual take-out, the old railroad bridge just west of Route 9. This area is privately owned, but access by car is permitted as long as cars are not parked near the water. Cedar Creek continues under the railroad bridge and soon over a small dam at Route 9. From this point the character of the river changes. Bulkheaded backyards and tidewater take over and soon give way to the marinas and powerboats of Barnegat Bay.

Canoeing Cedar Creek from Double Trouble is one of our

Looking down from the dam at the reservoir above Double Trouble. An easy portage on the right provides an opportunity to explore the many trails or just to take a short break from paddling.

View downstream from the bridge at Double Trouble—an excellent place to start a cruise. Cranberries and blueberries grow wild here, and many sandy roads and trails make hiking a pleasure.

On a hill overlooking the bogs, the old sorting house stands as a reminder of the once-thriving cranberry industry at Double Trouble.

A worker's cabin at Double Trouble State Park.

Just west of Route 9, this old railroad trestle marks a convenient take-out for trips from Double Trouble and Dover Forge.

Canoes awaiting their masters prior to the annual New Year's Day trip.

favorite excursions. We have been able to paddle it in every month of the year and have always found the scenery beautiful and the tea-colored water plentiful. Cranberry plants grow wild on the banks of the river, and in autumn the ripe berries are easy to spot and pick. Lunch spots are numerous, and the occasional swimming hole allows for a refreshing summertime dip.

The Delaware and Raritan Canal

$\mathcal{J}$n this day of tremendous mechanical earthmoving equipment, the job of digging a ditch forty-four miles long, eight feet deep, and seventy-five feet wide would not offer a serious challenge to an engineering firm. Imagine, if you can, doing such a job without the aid of any mechanical equipment—just pick and shovel, wheelbarrow, and horse-drawn scrapers. It seems impossible, but that was how the Delaware and Raritan Canal was built more than 150 years ago.

Hundreds of Irish immigrants who put their strong backs into that big job lie buried along the banks of the canal. They were victims of a cholera epidemic, and their only monument was the successful accomplishment of their great task.

The Delaware and Raritan Canal was completed and opened for business in the summer of 1834, and for almost a hundred years it was a very busy and important part of New Jersey's transportation facilities. During the years of its active commercial use, hundreds of mule-drawn barges and, in the spring and fall, elegant yachts made their leisurely way through this waterway. It was a boon to the pleasure-craft owners, as it provided a quicker and safer journey to and from Florida. The sound of the tin fish horns, blowing for the locks and bridges, is heard no more. Now only canoes and other nonmotorized craft use the canal.

Once kept free of trees and brush to enable the mules to tow the barges without snagging the tow lines, the canal bank is now almost completely overgrown. Because of this the canal now looks more like a natural stream than an artificial waterway.

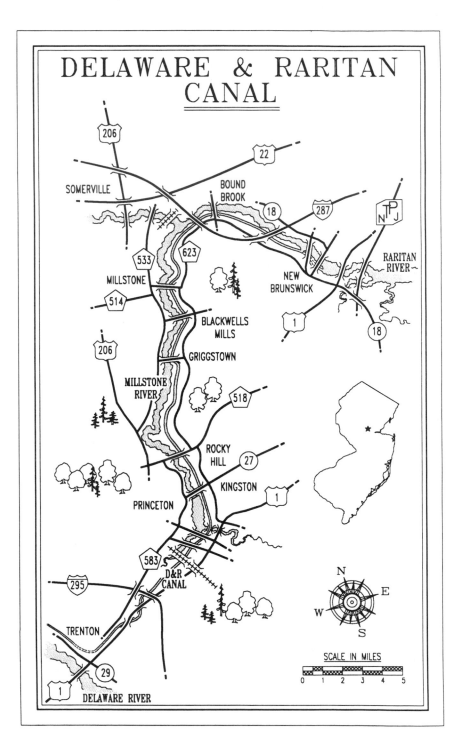

DELAWARE & RARITAN CANAL

SCALE IN MILES

0 1 2 3 4 5

The Delaware and Raritan Canal, like others built during the early years of the nineteenth century, was a result of the ever-increasing desire for better and faster transportation of goods. Prior to the opening of the canal most of the heavy tonnage carried between Philadelphia and New York was shipped by sailing vessels over the open sea. Due to weather conditions and lack of fair sailing breezes, it sometimes required as long as two weeks for the voyage. With the canal, a safe, all-weather route was available that required only two or three days. Through the lower reaches of the Raritan River to New Brunswick, then by the canal to the Delaware River at Bordentown, the barges could operate twenty-four hours a day. Furthermore, the earlier stage roads were over-burdened with traffic, and the canal helped relieve that situation.

Few people realize that in its heyday our canal carried a greater tonnage than did the more famous Erie Canal in New York State. At its peak in 1859, the Delaware and Raritan handled over two-and-one-half million tons of cargo. Naturally, this big volume of

Blackwells Mills with old bridge tender's house.

The former Atlantic Terra Cotta Company, between Griggstown and Kingston, was served by the canal and the railroad. Tiles for various buildings around the country were produced here, including those for the Woolworth building in New York City.

business benefited all the towns along the route. It was a great factor in the development of the economy of the entire state of New Jersey and of the ports of New York and Philadelphia.

To ensure a plentiful supply of water by gravity, a dam was built across the Delaware River at Raven Rock, and a feeder canal was dug parallel to the river from above the dam to Trenton. This provided a never-failing supply of water for the entire canal. The feeder was also used to carry coal from the Pennsylvania mines to the New York and Philadelphia areas.

All commercial activity on the canal ceased in 1932, just about a hundred years after it was opened to traffic. The canal is now owned by the state of New Jersey and is maintained by the New Jersey Water Supply Authority in the Department of Environmental Protection as a source of potable and industrial water for com-

Large kiln of the Atlantic Terra Cotta Company in the Kingston area.

munities along the way between Trenton and New Brunswick. The Division of Parks and Forestry administers the recreational resources such as Bull's Island Park at the head of the feeder and towpath improvement and maintenance for cyclists, picnickers, and canoeists.

After improvements to the towpath were started many years ago, there was a noticeable increase in the use of the canal and its facilities. On any weekend it is not unusual to see fifty or more canoes on the canal between Millstone and Kingston.

Today the canal offers endless opportunities for quiet cruising, away from the noise and tension of the highways. Over sixty miles of clean water in the feeder and main canal offer the canoeist one of the finest recreational waterways in the entire country. For example, we have on many trips started at Trenton and cruised for a day or two to the head of the feeder at Raven Rock. At that point we usually carry over into the Delaware River for the faster return trip by river. Both the feeder and the river have plenty of beautiful scenery and many things of historic interest to enjoy.

The first few miles of the feeder from Trenton are built-up and uninteresting, as that part is through the residential section of the city. It is better to start your cruise a few miles above, at Washington Crossing. Before embarking at that point, plan to spend an hour or so in the state parks on the New Jersey and the Pennsylvania sides. Enjoy the quiet sense of history that you will feel as you stand at the point where Washington and his Continental Army made their river crossing on that historic Christmas night in 1776. On the bank of the feeder, see the monument to John Honeyman, reputed to have been Washington's personal spy. Across the road and a bit above the feeder still stands the McKonkey House, where Washington and his men were given food and hot drinks before they started the march downriver on that very cold Christmas night.

From Trenton to Raven Rock, on the feeder, the Delaware River is never far away, and as Lambertville is approached, that fact is made evident by the roar of Wells Falls. At that point a carry around the lock is necessary. Pause a bit and enjoy these remnants of an earlier day. Until the 1950s most of the old locks were intact, and it was always a great thrill to sneak the canoe in with a barge and thus save a carry.

DELAWARE & RARITAN
FEEDER CANAL

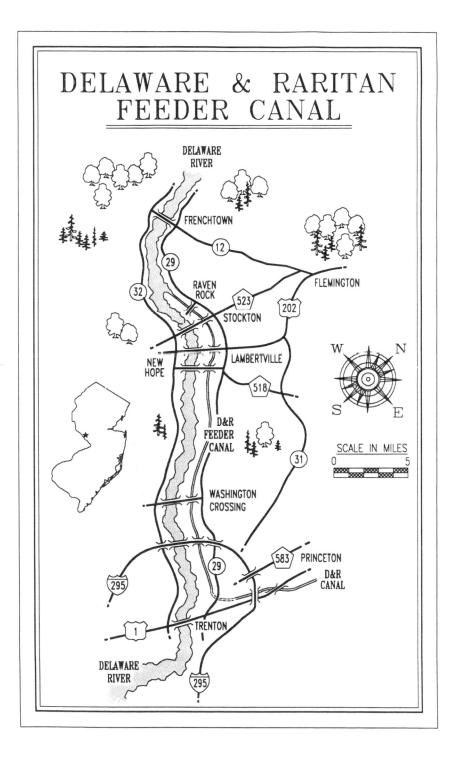

Most cruisers will end their first day's journey at Lambertville. Plenty of overnight accommodations are available, and you will enjoy spending an evening in this historic village. For those so inclined, the Bucks County Playhouse across the river in New Hope, an artsy, upscale tourist town, offers an excellent evening's entertainment.

From Lambertville to the end of the feeder, the countryside is less built-up and more natural. The hills of the Delaware valley become more prominent on that stretch of the feeder.

At Raven Rock the canoeist has two choices: to return to Trenton by way of the feeder, or to return by the river. One point of caution should be borne in mind if the river trip is decided upon:

Founded in 1903, the Mohawk Canoe Club, on the shore of the Delaware River in Stacy Park, Trenton, is one of the oldest active canoe clubs in the country. Unfortunately, in the summer of 1970, vandals destroyed the contents of the clubhouse and burned down the building.

Unless you are a fairly competent canoeist, the river journey may offer some hazards, depending upon the height of the water. The experienced paddler should not have any difficulty. Beginner or expert, do not attempt to run Wells Falls at Lambertville. It is an easy matter to carry your canoe around the falls on the New Jersey side of the river at that point or to complete the trip via the feeder.

A mile or so above Trenton is Scudders Falls; if you can swim, test your paddling skill there. It is a fast run of sometimes heavy water, but there are no rocks to upset the canoe.

For those who may wish to enjoy a series of afternoon journeys, we suggest Princeton as the starting point. The canal, Lake Carnegie, which adjoins it, and the upper Millstone are all readily accessible, and in fact a journey of several days may be started at that point. Cruising down Lake Carnegie, on through the Millstone River into the Raritan and on to New Brunswick, then returning to Princeton by canal requires several days.

During extremely hot days, the shaded reaches of Stony Brook

Looking east in the Princeton Turning Basin area, along the towpath and canal.

Old Steamboat Hotel in the Princeton Turning Basin area. A park with picnic tables and rest facilities is nearby.

(see the chapter "Small Streams") at the head of Lake Carnegie are enjoyable, as are the few miles of the wild, marsh-bordered areas of the upper Millstone, east of Route 1. That part of the river is teeming with all kinds of bird life, and the fall foliage is beautiful. The combination of the canal, Stony Brook, Lake Carnegie, the Millstone and Raritan rivers, the canal feeder, and the Delaware River provides an unsurpassed variety of canoeing opportunity. It is easy to get to any part of those waters, and trips can be planned as a series of weekends or days.

Unlike the rivers, which at times may be obstructed by fallen trees or too shallow to navigate, the canal is always a clean, open

Kingston locks and the lock tender's house. The locks are no longer in use and have been modified to serve as flood control gates. The lock tender's house is now a residence and canoe livery. A small building behind the house served as the first commercial telegraph station.

waterway. One may stop for a refreshing swim or a quiet rest anywhere along the towpath. One is expected, however, to observe the rules of good outdoorsmanship, doing no damage and leaving the area clean.

Along the route of the entire canal, one may still see the old stone and plaster houses where the lock and bridge tenders lived. Beside the lock tender's house at Kingston still stands a little frame building that was originally the tollhouse for the canal. It played a more important role than that, however: It was one of the first commercial installations of the Morse telegraph, which had first been put into operation a few years after the canal was opened for business. It was the principal means of communication along the entire canal.

Originally the locks were for the purpose of raising or lowering

Bridge tender's house at the site of a former swing bridge in Griggstown.

boats from one level to another. They have now been replaced by concrete spillways to keep the water level constant.

We enjoyed the many canoe rendezvous with our canoeing companions from our club at Bound Brook, many years ago. Each spring, during the boat-racing season on Lake Carnegie in May, we would get together on Friday evenings and, with duffel properly packed, start cruising up the canal. Our objective was Griggstown, fourteen miles away, which we would reach very late that night. These cruises were a lot of fun, as is always the case where ten or fifteen like-minded people get together. Camp would be made on the towpath at Griggstown, and before turning in we would enjoy an hour of campfire singing and talk.

Early in the morning we would embark for Princeton, reaching our campsite around noon, or at least in time to witness such classic events as the Carnegie or Childs Cup races on the lake. On Sunday we would cruise down the lake and through the Millstone

Griggstown bridge over canal and lock tender's house.

Looking west along the canal and towpath near the South Bound Brook lock.

and the Raritan, reaching our clubhouse sometime in the evening. We heartily recommend that some of our readers get together and revive those old-time affairs. You will be glad you did, and we suspect that it will become a habit. Unfortunately, camping is no longer permitted along the canal.

Despite the fact that all of the old sheer-leg swing bridges have been replaced by more modern structures to carry the heavier traffic of today, and although all the old locks have been replaced by less interesting spillways, one has the feeling, when cruising the canal today, of being back in an earlier century. The villages like Kingston, Griggstown, and East Millstone are still quiet little oases, little affected by the tension and hurry of modern civilization. Should you ever stop at Griggstown, for example, spend a few minutes walking around the village in the evening. Somehow, in

The towpath as seen between the canal (left) and the Raritan (right), near I–287.

such a place, one expects to hear mule bells and to see a canal barge come around the bend.

Perhaps the best way to get to know and love the canal is to plan a series of afternoon trips on various parts of it. You will soon discover the parts of the canal you like the best and can then plan more extensive trips as you become familiar with it.

Around the canal, as is true of any institution that has endured for over a century, many tales have developed. Some are true and some are otherwise. One of the old stories that has always intrigued us—and it happens to be true—is about the people who lived along a certain part of the canal in Trenton. Most of the houses had high wooden fences to keep children out of the canal. Someone had the happy inspiration of lining his fence with bottles. When the coal barges passed, the canallers just could not resist heaving coal at the bottles. Thus a winter's supply of coal was obtained without cost.

Another man hit upon a better idea. He chained a pet monkey

The canal as it crosses the Millstone above Lake Carnegie.

An old photograph of swing gates at the outlet lock in New Brunswick. They were removed years ago, and the tide from the Raritan River now ebbs and flows through the lower level of the canal.

to the fence and not only obtained all the coal he needed, but enough to sell to some of his neighbors as well.

Many such yarns are still told along the canal and in the villages along the way. Seek out the people who can tell them. Hearing the stories will give you a better picture of the canal and add considerably to your enjoyment of it.

The Great Egg Harbor River

$\mathcal{I}$n May, the shores of the Great Egg Harbor River are a riot of laurel, lupine, and water iris. In the fall, the shores are ablaze with a palette of color from swamp maples and alders. The holly, pines, and white, sandy shores make this beautiful river quite different from its sister Pine Barrens rivers.

The Great Egg Harbor River passes under Route 322 near the little hamlet of Penny Pot. As you approach the river, its wild beauty becomes evident. Close by is the best place to start your journey, as three branches join in the Penny Pot area, and the upper reaches of these branches are very wild, tangled, and rough to navigate. One branch, the Hospitality Branch, has its origins in a small pond south of Berlin in Camden County.

Atlantic County has provided an excellent launch site on 8th Street, just off Spur 561 where it separates from Route 322, or the Black Horse Pike as it is better known. The Atlantic County Park System has provided two other areas along the river to break up the trip as well as to allow an opportunity to explore the remains of Weymouth Furnace and the Lake Lenape area.

Particularly from Penny Pot to Weymouth, the river may sometimes be a bit difficult to run due to fallen trees and other obstructions. If the stream below Weymouth is shallow, as it sometimes is in the summer, the cruise can be ended at Weymouth, where it is easy to get out of the river and to the road.

For those who may prefer to spend a day paddling or sailing on Lake Lenape, which is that part of the river from the dam at Mays Landing upstream for a mile or so, we suggest launching

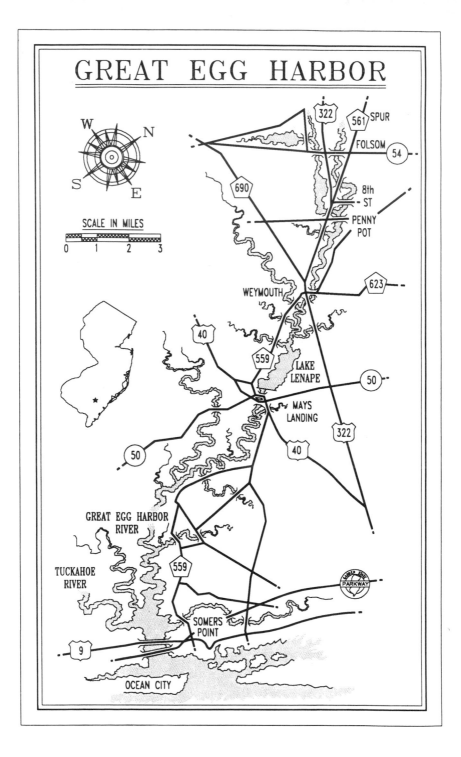

GREAT EGG HARBOR

The small beginning of the Great Egg Harbor River near its source below Berlin. From this point to Penny Pot the river is too difficult for comfortable canoe cruising.

*Most trips start from this new launch area pro-
vided by the Atlantic County Park System,
near the hamlet of Penny Pot.*

your canoe at the Atlantic County Park access area. A day on the lake, when there is not too much wind, is delightful.

For bird lovers, poking in and out of the many bays along the shores will be rewarding. All kinds of birds are found, and in fact you may be lucky enough, as we have been, to spot ospreys, wood ducks, and prothonotary warblers.

One might also like to camp along the river and make a two-day journey out of it. Winding River Campground, a few miles above Mays Landing, is a delightful, wooded campground along the river. Canoe rentals are available here, or, if you provide your own canoe, arrangements can be made for transportation back to your car. Otherwise, cruisers have to end their trips at Weymouth or continue all the way to Mays Landing. The Mays Landing take-out is at the Atlantic County Park System Lake Lenape access area.

On a weekend canoe trip we retraced part of the route from Sicklerville to Mays Landing described by Harry van Dyke in a story, "Between the Lupine and the Laurel," published in 1907.

What could be a better family outing than an early fall cruise down the Great Egg Harbor River?

Van Dyke wrote of canoeing with four Quaker companions down a "mysterious" South Jersey river, the name of which he did not disclose, as he believed that "the name of the hiding-place should not be published, lest the careless, fad-following crowd should flock thither and spoil it." We do not feel as van Dyke did about such things—they should be shared and enjoyed by all—and we quote a part of his description of the river, which is still very much as it was when he "discovered" it:

It was thus that my four friends—Friends in creed as well as in deed—told me . . . of their secret find of a little river in South Jersey, less than an hour from Philadelphia, where one could float in a canoe through mile after mile of unbroken woodland, and camp at night in a bit of wilderness as wildly fair as when the wigwams of the Lenni-Lenape were hidden among its pine groves. The Friends said they "had a concern" to guide me to their delectable retreat and they hoped "the way would open" for me to come. . . .

Our "earthly labor" began again when we started down the stream; for now we had fairly entered the long strip of wilderness which curtains its winding course. On either hand the thickets came down so close to the water that there were no banks left; just woods and water blending; and the dark topaz current swirling and gurgling through a clump of bushes or round the trunk of a tree, as if it did not care what path it took, so long as it got through. Alders and pussy-willows, viburnums, clethras, choke-cherries, swamp maples, red birches, and all sorts of trees and shrubs that are water loving, made an intricate labyrinth for the stream to thread; and through the tangle, cat-briers, black-berries, fox grapes, and poison ivy were interlaced. . . .

It was no easy task to guide the boat down the swift current, for it was bewilderingly crooked, twisting and turning upon itself in a way that would make the fair Meander look like a straight line. . . .

A handcrafted scoop with which cranberries were harvested until machines came into use.

How charming was the curve of that brown, foam-flecked stream, as it rushed swiftly down, from pool to pool, under the ancient, overhanging elms, willows and sycamores.

In 1935, as we were doing the research and photography for the first edition of this book, we set out to locate van Dyke's "mysterious" river. We finally discovered it, despite the difficulty he had created by using such names as Hummington for Hammonton and Watermouth for Weymouth—van Dyke had been cruising the Great Egg Harbor River.

It was a lovely May day when we loaded our little fifteen-foot, forty-five-pound canoe on the top of our station wagon to follow the route of van Dyke and his Quaker companions. It was apparent that we were not going to be able to paddle near the source of the river. We did manage to follow it by car, launching the canoe

The old teak dam at Penny Pot, recently reconstructed. The teak was salvaged from eighteenth-century warships.

at Penny Pot for the start of the cruise. At this point the river was narrow, with swift-flowing water and foliage overhead forming a green arch. Occasionally we had to carry over or around fallen trees.

The many cranberry bogs in this vicinity reminded us that our traditional feast of turkey and cranberries was passed along to the Europeans by the Indians, according to legend. Whether that is so or not, it is a fact that this region was plentifully supplied with wild cranberries and turkeys at one time.

The wild and swampy areas of the upper part of the Great Egg Harbor River are ideal for the cultivation of cranberries, and they used to be the principal money crop of this region. From December to April the bogs are flooded to protect the vines from frost, and in the spring the water is drawn off. In early summer the berries begin to show, and by harvest time in September, they are very colorful.

During one of our river exploration trips that summer, as we were launching our canoe near the dam at Penny Pot, we met the owner of the adjoining land, Mr. John Kinney, who expressed great interest in our trip. When he learned that we were gathering material for a book, he gave us some new information about the locality. "This place," remarked Mr. Kinney, "is known as Penny Pot, and it was so named in 1686 by the first settlers because it resembled the countryside of their native home in England."

We inquired about the purpose of the dam and were told that it was originally used as a cranberry dam and later to furnish power for a gristmill. An unusual fact about the dam is the material of which it was made. The cost of lumber for such a dam would ordinarily be about $600, but this one has timber in it that had at the time a market value of about $75,000. It seems a friend of Mr. Kinney sent him truckloads of teak timber, salvaged from old warships, when the friend heard lumber was needed for a new dam. It is doubtless the only dam in the country built of that costly wood. Although the dam has been rebuilt, much of the original teak can still be seen.

Five minutes after leaving the dam, the river became a wilderness: trees crowding the stream, in places actually shutting out all sunlight; the shores a profusion of lupine, holly, and laurel. The

Above, the old Methodist Church in Weymouth. Left, one of several unusual iron grave markers in the churchyard. This one, cast at the nearby Weymouth Iron Works, honors the memory of Rosana Ireland Babington, who died in 1825 at the age of eighteen months.

Remains of a paper mill that was built on the foundations of the early nineteenth-century Weymouth Furnace. Iron was produced from bog ore mined in the surrounding swamps and brought to the furnace by small barges poled along canals. Weymouth Furnace cast cannons and balls for the War of 1812 and the first iron pipe for the City of Philadelphia. The paper mill was erected here shortly after the furnace closed in 1862. All operations ceased about 1887.

pine trees and a combination of white sand and clay along the shores were in vivid contrast to the foliage overhead. The journey from Penny Pot to Weymouth was one of endless beauty, with few signs of civilization along the way. It seems incredible that such a wilderness could have been found within thirty miles of Philadelphia. Today many more signs of civilization are evident, but it is remarkable that so few buildings or other evidence of the population explosion are to be seen.

It is not possible for the motorist to get to the river at many points between Penny Pot and Weymouth, but the general character of the river may be seen by looking upstream and downstream from the bridge at Weymouth.

The village of Weymouth itself is worth a thorough inspection. The places of interest and the colorful history of this one-time thriving community are fascinating. The visitor will find a tangle of vine-covered ruins that were once the scene of industrial activity. Under the ruins of the paper mill in the state park on the river stood the Weymouth Iron Works, built in 1801. The Weymouth Company's extensive landholdings of iron bogs, timberlands for charcoal, worker housing, and other facilities made this one of the largest operations of its kind in the Pine Barrens. During the War of 1812, grapeshot and cannonballs for the U.S. Navy were produced in this forge.

The ore was bog iron from local pits, and in smelting it eight wagonloads of charcoal were used for a single charge of the furnace. It was a crude but effective process, and from such simple

An unusual view of the old millrace at Weymouth, as seen from a canoe while cruising down the Great Egg Harbor River.

beginnings came our present-day complicated steel industry. Not far from the furnace one may find the remains of the roadbed that was once a mule-powered railroad, used to haul products to Mays Landing.

Nearby is the famous Indian Spring, which has flowed steadily through wet and dry seasons for centuries. It is still the source of drinking water for people of the vicinity. On a high bank overlooking the river formerly stood the old manor house, which was built in the eighteenth century. Its entire frame was of local cedar.

In late May the entire river is a scene of unsurpassed beauty. Miles of blossoming laurel with a background of stately pines unfold before the canoeist. On a quiet day the entire scene is duplicated in mirror form beneath the canoe.

About halfway between Penny Pot and Mays Landing the river widens out, with large areas of backwaters on either shore, offering endless opportunities for exploration. The river bottom is of pure white sand, delightful to walk upon in your bare feet. Deer and other game are plentiful.

The canopy of maples and other deciduous trees makes for a beautiful cruise throughout the year, especially in the spring and autumn.

The
Hackensack

Although the Hackensack River today may not offer as much canoeable water as many other New Jersey rivers, one may still find many miles on which a canoe may be used. The valley through which the river flows is rich in history.

One fall afternoon, while cruising down the Hackensack River from Old Tappan, our thoughts were on the subject of the Indian history of the country through which we were passing. The Lenape Indians knew this stream as "the river of many bends," and they had many villages along its shores before the settlement of the Hackensack valley by the Dutch. The name Lenape means "the first people," although no one knows how many years they inhabited the area.

As we paddled around a bend in the river, we were startled to see what appeared to be a full-blooded Indian launching a birch-bark canoe. Our surprise was shared by the young Indian, who was equally startled to see us swinging downstream in our Canadian cruising canoe.

We went ashore and spent a very enjoyable afternoon on the site of one of the early settlements of the Lenape, where a project was underway to reproduce an actual Indian village. This project was originally intended as a permanent exhibit and was to be the setting for lectures, craft demonstrations, and a series of authentic motion pictures depicting the way of life of the Lenape. Difficulties of various sorts caused the plan to be abandoned, but during that first summer of construction, ceremonies and dances had been presented every Sunday afternoon by a group of twenty or so Indians from Long Island. A deep interest in the life of the New

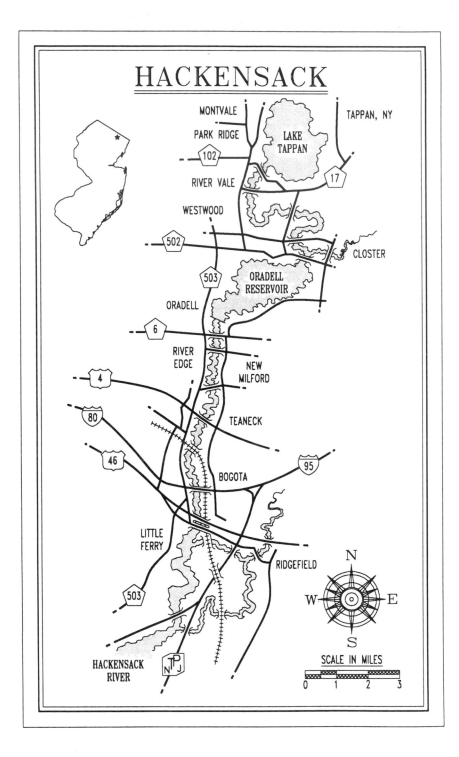

HACKENSACK

MONTVALE

TAPPAN, NY

PARK RIDGE

LAKE TAPPAN

102

RIVER VALE

17

WESTWOOD

502

CLOSTER

503

ORADELL RESERVOIR

ORADELL

6

RIVER EDGE

NEW MILFORD

4

80

TEANECK

46

95

BOGOTA

LITTLE FERRY

RIDGEFIELD

503

HACKENSACK RIVER

NJTP

N

W   E

S

SCALE IN MILES

0   1   2   3

The river at the River Vale–Old Tappan line. Surrounded by busy highways and homes, it nevertheless appears like a stream in a less populated part of the state.

Jersey Indians came naturally to the project's sponsors, Mrs. Vivienne Paul and her father Parselles Cole, descendants of the Campbell family, which manufactured wampum for trade with the Indians.

Little has been written about this interesting phase of Hackensack valley history, originally centered on what is now Park Ridge, known in colonial days as Pascack. For many years the Campbell Brothers manufactured wampum here in a small factory and traded with the Indians at the John Astor Trading Post nearby. The post was originally a blockhouse during the Indian Wars and later, during the Revolution, a fort. There members of the Astor family began trading wampum for furs, and from that small beginning enlarged their operations into their huge northwestern fur empire. A Campbell operated the last wampum factory at New Milford until the middle of the nineteenth century.

Dutch settlers first arrived in the Hackensack valley in the early years of the seventeenth century, and some of the sandstone houses they built at that time are still standing. One of the most notable of the early Dutch homes is the Zabriskie house in River

Edge, which was built in the mid-eighteenth century. John Zabriskie, its builder, was an active Tory, and during the Revolution his
home was confiscated by the government. After the war it was
presented to Baron von Steuben, the drillmaster of the Continental Army, in recognition of his services. It is now a museum, open
to the public for a small fee.

A small park just below Lake Tappan has been dedicated to the
memory of another episode in the Revolution. In 1778 over a
hundred dragoons of the Continental Army commanded by Colonel George Baylor were surprised in their bivouac on the bank of
the Hackensack by a much larger force of British, who wiped out
over half of Baylor's command. The engagement has since been
referred to by historians as the Baylor Massacre. Except for stu-
dents of history, few people remembered much of that event until
a dramatic discovery of the actual site of the massacre was made
in 1969.

The details of how that important excavation disclosed the

*A group of Indians in front of a bark-covered
long house they erected on the shore of the
river during the 1960s. Here ceremonial
dances and craft demonstrations were held all
summer.*

This typical early Dutch house on DeWolf Road in Old Tappan is believed to have been built in 1704 by Cosyn Haring It has been continuously occupied by descendants of the original owner.

mass graves of the dragoons is well documented in a booklet entitled *1778: The Massacre of Baylor's Dragoons.* A copy may be obtained by writing to the Board of Chosen Freeholders, Bergen County, Hackensack, New Jersey.

During the early days of the colonies the Hackensack was an important commercial stream, as in fact it still is. Old records indicate that this river was second only to the lower Raritan in the volume of freight carried on it. From the records we find that "in 1750 boats and large sloops were sailing daily in summer up and down the Hackensack, carrying freight for the settlements and plantations along the banks."

At that time the main road through the valley was the Old Tappan Road, which followed the river into New York State. It is now known variously as River Street, Kinderkamack Road, and Tappan Road. Today one can drive along the river on this road into New York to see evidence of our past in the town of Tappan. It was there can provide an interesting visit. The museum is only a five-minute drive from the river.

This river became an important source of fresh water for the city of Hackensack in 1869, when the Hackensack Water Company was formed. Water was initially pumped out of the Hackensack into a brick-lined reservoir and then allowed to flow downhill to the city. By the end of the nineteenth century, the need for water in the surrounding communities had increased to the point that the Oradell Reservoir was built in 1902. This reservoir was adequate until the post–World War II building boom, coupled with a drought in the 1960s, initiated the building of Lake Tappan in 1967. With a fifty-five-foot dam, Lake Tappan adds 45 percent to the storage capacity of the river and covers 1255 acres in River Vale and Old Tappan. Today, the Hackensack Water Company provides water to over seventy communities in the area.

The amount of Hackensack waters open to canoeists is limited by the dams and the prohibition of boating on the Lake Tappan and Oradell reservoirs. However, canoeists may use several miles of the river below Lake Tappan and the lower reaches of the tidal water during periods of high-water slack. Before launching a ca-

The Hackensack below the lower end of the Oradell Reservoir.

The river from the old iron bridge in River Edge, at high tide.

noe, it would be a good idea to inquire locally whether canoeing is allowed.

As far back as the early years of the twentieth century a plan to build a dam in the vicinity of Teaneck to stop tidal flow in the Hackensack above that point was seriously considered. As with many such plans, there was a great deal of talk, and then the plans were forgotten. They were revived about 1935, again discussed at some length, and again tabled.

Once, over a period of four Saturdays, local Girl Scouts and other civic-minded people lifted and hauled away over sixty truckloads of debris from the Hackensack, including washing machines, steel drums, refrigerators, and even whole auto engines.

With the pressure to clean up New York Bay, all tidal areas in the Hackensack River have improved. One of the important factors for preserving the meadowlands of the lower Hackensack has been the effort to make the area more hospitable to shorebirds. Wildlife management areas and bird sanctuaries provide bird-watchers an opportunity to see stilt sandpipers, Hudsonian god-

The salt-marsh grass that covers the meadows along the Hackensack estuary may be seen waving in the breeze along the shore.

wits, American avocets, and many migratory waterfowl species. Shorebirds abound during May, and again in late August and early September. Access to these meadowlands exists via private boat launches at the end of Paterson Plank Road in Carlstadt and at the end of Mill Ridge Road in Secaucus.

Some years ago, as we were paddling above Hackensack, we were hailed by a lady on the shore. She told us that seeing us swing by in our canoe reminded her of an earlier day. With a sparkle in her eye she told us about the old Kinderkamack Canoe Club and how they had steak and fish dinners at their clubhouse above Oradell once each month. They would launch their canoes at their backyard and paddle seven miles up to the club in the evening, returning to their homes late at night.

Perhaps it is wishful thinking on our part and of others who remember the Hackensack many, many years ago, but we would like to see that river again filled with canoes and other small craft.

The Manasquan River and Inlet

The Manasquan River was not included as a chapter in the earliest editions of this book because it was so full of trees and brush that canoeing was possible only on small sections here and there. In 1969, under the leadership of the members of the Murray Hill Canoe Club, the Wall Township and Manasquan Kiwanis clubs, Boy Scout Post 197, and the Monmouth County Park System, several weekends were spent clearing the river from Ardena (Havens Bridge Road) down. It was a terrific job, as trees with a diameter of two feet had to be cut and hauled out of the river.

Despite the clearing job, the Manasquan is blocked again above Howell High School. Every spring new blockages appear downstream from the high school and the Howell Golf Course; however, resourceful canoeists find their way over or around the obstacles. A few public-spirited individuals carry bowsaws occasionally and cut through the serious blockages. The reason for the many blockages is the soft loam of the banks, which is easily washed from under the tree roots, causing the trees to drop into the river.

Water levels in the Manasquan vary greatly depending on local rainfall. When it is over its banks, the river can be treacherous. It moves slowly around the trees that are outside its banks, but where the banks are high or a bridge looms ahead, the water moves swiftly and can trap a canoe under fallen tree branches or against a bridge abutment. When the water is low, be prepared to squeeze under many of the fallen trees that span the stream and to drag or pole the canoe across sand bars.

A new reservoir has been built upstream from the Howell Golf

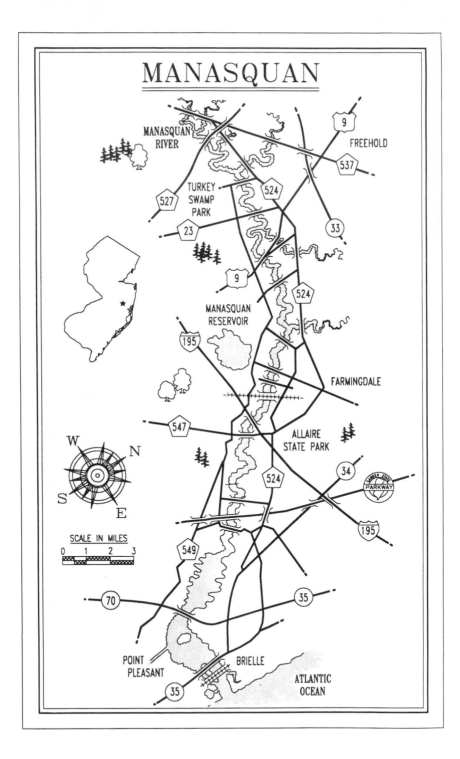

Course. At this writing it is still filling with water. It will supplement the supply of potable water for this fast-growing area of the state. Water is drawn out of the river just above Hospital Bridge and pumped several miles upstream to the reservoir. Water will be released from the reservoir and could provide a more uniform flow in the river.

Just below the water plant is a dam with the shape of a shallow V. Canoeists may be tempted to run the dam if the water is fairly high, but the Monmouth County Park Service prohibits this. At low water corrugated iron edges stick up just below the V, forming a jagged wall that threatens canoes and passengers alike.

Day trips may be started at the Iron Bridge at Howell Golf Course. The river is difficult but passable in the stretch between here and Route 547. This area is easily blocked by fallen trees, and it is shallow during periods of low water. Route 547 crosses the river at Squankum. This spot may also be reached by road between the divided lanes of Route 547, making it a convenient

Tree bridges and other obstacles are formed when the soft soil of the banks gives way.

place to enter the river. There is a dam at this point that is a challenge to canoeists and is also a favorite spot for fishermen. Most canoeists carry around the dam and make apologies to the fishermen. Other canoeists shoot the dam and make apologies to the fishermen.

From here it is an easy half-hour paddle to Allaire Park. Canoeists may stop at the park to picnic and enjoy the interesting restoration of a typical bog-iron operation, which includes the Deserted Village. In addition to the craft interpreters at the many shops in the village, there is now a reconstructed narrow-gauge railway on which one may ride on weekends. The park also provides musical programs on some Sundays in the summer.

To continue the river journey it is about an hour's paddle, depending upon conditions, from Allaire Park through Spring Meadow Golf Course, past the pumping station and Hospital Road to Brice Park. This park, just east of where the Garden State Parkway crosses the Manasquan, was once a convenient place to dis-

The new dam and pumping station along the Manasquan River downstream from Allaire supply water to the Manasquan Reservoir.

The Howell Furnace in Allaire State Park is the only one of the bog iron furnaces left intact. It was in operation until 1848.

*The restored general store, which was the com-
pany store during the heyday of Allaire.*

embark. Now, unfortunately, the concrete launch ramp has been
washed away, and launching or landing of watercraft is not permitted. The road serving the park crosses the Manasquan less than
a quarter mile farther down, and while there are several ways to
take out at this road, none of them is really convenient.

It should be apparent from the preceding description that this
is not one of the typical Jersey rivers that permit uninterrupted
paddling for a full day. However, that is possible if one continues
through the saltwater inlet as far as Brielle, on Route 70. To try
that, one should be waterwise enough to anticipate sudden squalls
and high seas. On a calm day without a headwind the journey
through the inlet to Brielle, or for that matter to the sea at Point
Pleasant, can be delightful.

Since 1970 the Monmouth County Park System has spon-
sored a canoe race on the Manasquan River, usually in early May.
It begins at the Iron Bridge at Howell Golf Course. The race traverses the tricky upper part of the river, negotiates the dam at

Squankum, passes through the beautiful scenery of Allaire and around the water plant dam above Hospital Road, and finishes in tidal water at Brice Park. The many obstacles on the Manasquan add interest and challenge to the race, and the dam at Squankum can provide good photographic opportunities. The Monmouth County Park System will rent canoes for the race. Also, there is a canoe livery on Yellow Brook Road, south of the high school and just north of the railroad crossing.

For those not too interested in canoeing, particularly through the obstacle course of the fallen timber, we suggest exploring the river by car, camping overnight, and spending several hours in Allaire Park. A general impression of the river may be gained via the many roads that cross it; a drive along Route 524 to Manasquan and the shore is a delightful way to spend a day or a weekend. The booklet on Allaire Park, which may be obtained free at the park, is very informative and will help you plan your journey of exploration on or along the river.

Our first visit to the then deserted village, many years before it

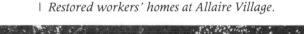

| *Restored workers' homes at Allaire Village.*

The mill pond which supplies water for turning the wheels of the gristmill and other works in the iron village at Allaire State Park.

was restored as one of the most interesting of New Jersey's state parks, made a deep and lasting impression on us. During that visit, before the restoration in 1959 by the Division of Parks and Forestry, the ruins of the village were somewhat spooky and mysterious. It reminded us of some of the western ghost towns we had visited. The several buildings still standing had that forlorn air common to such places. The little church, the smithy, the country store, and the old post office were reminders of the once prosperous mill village.

As we sat on the shore of the Manasquan River near the village, we tried to visualize what the village must have been like in its heyday. At the height of the bog-iron operations, between the years 1834 and 1837, over five hundred people were employed here. From all accounts the workers were well housed in pleasant company houses, used the facilities of the large company store, and lived a generally happy life.

As with most of the little rivers of New Jersey, there are many

The village post office in Allaire State Park is open to visitors.

Restored chapel at Allaire. Weddings are still performed here.

Standard-gauge rails carry a freight line over the Manasquan.

tales about the Manasquan. It seems that one day several men were working at the salt works on the shore of the inlet, and they were besieged by hungry mosquitoes. In desperation the workers crawled under a large iron kettle to escape the pests. The mosquitoes immediately began drilling through the kettle, and, as each proboscis appeared on the inside of the kettle, the workmen would strike it with their hammers, riveting it fast. Finally, when a number had been hammered to the inside of the kettle, the mosquitoes flew off with it, after which the remainder of the swarm made short work of the men. We like the yarn but hasten to point out as good Jerseyans that things like that happened only before the establishment of New Jersey's state and county mosquito control commissions.

Another bit of folklore adds to the charm of the area. The tribes of the Lenape from as far away as Minisink Island on the upper Delaware River used to make an annual pilgrimage to the shore at Point Pleasant to feast on shellfish. It was in connection with those affairs that the Indians named the river and inlet. They called it Manatahasquahan, meaning the place where they left their squaws while the male members of the tribes gathered the shellfish. They loved this river and inlet and paddled their canoes on it as we do today.

Each year in September the people of Point Pleasant hold a community celebration to mark those early journeys to their seaside town. To the Indians, Point Pleasant was a favorite place by the sea, as it is for millions of annual visitors today.

The Maurice

The Maurice River offers a wide variety of beauty and many places of interest to explorers of the little streams of New Jersey. Like most South Jersey rivers, its actual beginning is hard to find. There are four branches—two start near Glassboro, another north of Clayton, and a fourth near Cross Keys. The last is known as Scotland Run. The two western branches come together a short distance below Franklinville and form the Maurice proper. Despite the spelling of the name, local folks pronounce it as if it were spelled "Morris." A few miles below Franklinville, at Malaga, Scotland Run adds its flow to the main stream.

The motorist will find this river fairly easy to explore, as it is a simple matter to get to any part of it. Canoeists, however, should confine their cruising to the part between Malaga or Willow Grove and Millville. It is of course possible to paddle a canoe all the way to Delaware Bay, but the tide and other conditions make the river less attractive below Millville.

One of the unusual features of this river is Union Lake, which was created by a dam at Millville. The water of the stream is backed up into a lake nearly four miles long, said to be the largest man-made lake in New Jersey. The uneven shores, the high cliffs of clay on the west shore, and the little islands combine to make this an attractive lake. Unfortunately, Union Lake was recently closed to clean up asbestos contamination, and it is not expected to reopen before 1997.

At the head of the stream in Glassboro one may still find evidence of the one-time prosperous industry of glass blowing. This industry had its start in America over two hundred years ago at

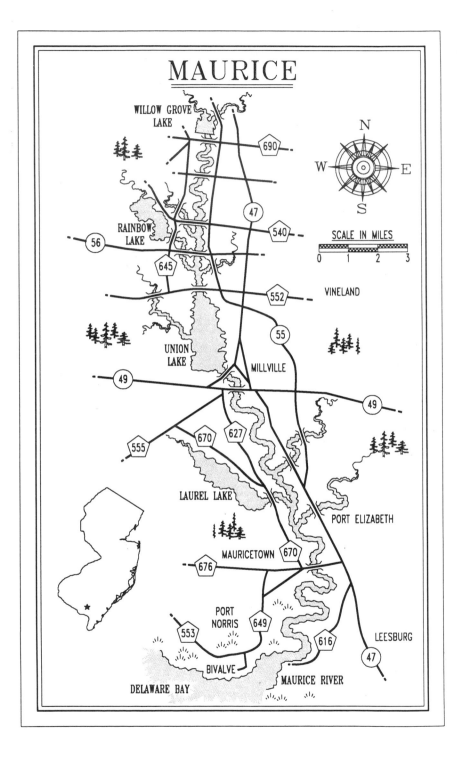

The railroad trestle below Route 540 is located in one of the few developed areas of the river.

Alloway, and shortly after the Revolution was moved to Glassboro, where it was carried on until the 1930s. The famous Wistar and Stanger glass had its early beginnings nearby, and the surrounding countryside is filled with the descendants of the Germans who founded this great industry in America.

On some parts of the upper reaches of the four branches of the Maurice are still found a few small dams, built a century or more ago to flood bogs and to supply power for the early gristmills. Above the dams are little lakes, some of which are remarkably beautiful sheets of water. For example, above the dam at Fries Mill on Scotland Run is an area of perfectly blue water, an unusual sight in this part of New Jersey, where most of the water is amber-colored. This lake is backed with acres of cedars and pines, which provide a rich contrast to and enhance the natural beauty of the blue water and of the skies reflected in it. It is such unexpected bits of loveliness that make the exploration of our rivers so delightful an experience.

From Malaga, where many cruisers start their journey, to the lake west of Willow Grove the Maurice runs fast—six miles or

more an hour at times. The speed of the foam-flecked amber water, rushing the canoeist around the bends and calling for occasional fast work with the paddle, provides a real thrill. As the
stream merges into the lake, the journey is slowed down a bit, but
soon after the dam at the foot of the lake is portaged, the speed of
the water increases again.

Many parties start their journey at this point, obtaining canoes
at Millville or carrying their own on top of their cars. By road the
distance to Millville is not over ten miles, but by water it is more
than twice that. Although the fast-running water enables one to
make the voyage to the head of Union Lake in an afternoon if
necessary, it is better to plan to devote a whole day, allowing for
stops to enjoy the woods and colorful foliage. In places the cedars
and pines form a solid green arch overhead, sometimes coming
down so close to the water that they make it difficult to get
through. On the upper river particularly, it is like emerging from
a tunnel to pass from the heavily forested area to the sunlit part of

*This beautiful crescent sand beach a few miles
above Union Lake makes an excellent spot to
stop for lunch or a swim.*

The dam below Route 540 has a lip and is best carried around on the right.

Oyster boats moored at Port Norris on the lower Maurice, as seen several decades ago. During the peak of the oyster trade, when all the boats depended on sail, hundreds of boats like these were in service.

the stream, with the bright sun of early summer dancing on the water. Everywhere the odor of white cedar fills the air.

Southwest of Vineland the river widens and soon changes character. The close intimacy of the little stream hemmed in by the crowding forest gives way to the sandy shores of Union Lake. The flood of cedar water is lost in the larger area of the blue water of the lake. A few small islands help give the impression of a natural lake, as do the sand beaches along its shores. On the east shore are many summer cottages and the usual recreational facilities, but they do not detract from the natural charm of the lake itself. Motorists may drive across the head and the foot of the lake, but it is necessary to seek out the roads through the woods to get to the more isolated parts of the shore.

At the lower end of the lake, cruisers must decide whether to terminate their trip or face a long carry around the dam and mills and then buck the tide of the lower river. There is plenty of interest below this point, but the comparatively uninteresting miles of salt marsh that line the shores make it advisable to finish the exploration along the river to Delaware Bay by car.

Below Millville the river again changes character. It is difficult to believe that the stream is the same one that begins at Glassboro. There are many scenes reminiscent of Gloucester, Massachusetts, along the part of the river that extends from Millville to the bay.

On the way to Bivalve are such places as Mauricetown, Port Norris, Buckshutem, Port Elizabeth, and others with names of English origin. Here and there stands a red-brick house of the colonial period. From Port Elizabeth famous clipper ships sailed out over the seven seas in the mid-nineteenth century. The development of railroads and modern highways has done much to spoil the charm of this community, but many of the early buildings remain. The old church, built in 1827, is surrounded by a cemetery that dates back to 1786. In years past in the neighborhood of Mauricetown one could see miles of dikes built by early settlers to reclaim the rich bottomland. Today most of the dikes are in disrepair, and the river has reclaimed much of the farmland. One last diked farm remains with about a mile of dike, a brick farmhouse and a barn; it is run by twin sisters who have retired to their family homestead to become the third generation to farm this land.

At Bivalve, where the Maurice ends its journey to the sea, there is a great deal to interest the visitor. The name of the town is obviously derived from its one-time chief industry. Out in Delaware Bay were the great oyster beds, which were recognized as an important natural resource as early as 1719. To prevent their spoilage, regulatory laws were passed early in the nineteenth century. As recently as 1950 the oyster harvesting and processing industry in Bivalve and vicinity carried a capital investment that ran into millions of dollars. In the early years of the century most of the oyster boats were under sail, and until 1945 dredging in the seed beds was permitted only by sailboats.

Around 1957, a deadly disease called MSX attacked the oyster beds and reduced the harvest to practically nothing. Attempts to control the parasite have so far been ineffective, and oystering in the area is essentially ended. In addition, recent warm winters have allowed a new parasite, Dermo, to move in from southern waters, and the dream of the oyster industry in Delaware Bay returning to its glory days seems very far away.

During a tour many years ago we were shown the great shucking and packing sheds in which the oysters were received, counted, and shucked for shipment. The shells were conveyed to large piles outside to be sold later. Today one of the shucking sheds remains in business by bringing in oysters from Long Island Sound.

To us the most fascinating feature of our visit was the oyster museum. Here are displayed many specimens of marine life, bottles, and branches of trees to which the oyster attaches itself, along with many other marine oddities. It is decidedly worth a visit.

The Delaware Bay Schooner Project, the brainchild of a young woman named Meghan Wren, is devoted to restoring an old, eighty-five-foot-long wooden oyster boat. Fewer than two dozen of the original oyster boats still exist, none of them intact. Hundreds of volunteers have been attracted to her weekend "work parties." Her eventual plan is to turn the boat into a traveling classroom under sail on the Delaware estuary, where children and others can learn of the bay's abundant resources and its maritime heritage. The Schooner Center in Port Norris is the headquarters

Reflections along the shore of the lower Maurice.

of this project, and there is a small exhibition there that chronicles the maritime tradition of Delaware Bay.

While the last few miles of the Maurice are tidal and not well suited to canoe cruising, the reader may want to make arrangements with one of the power boat owners at Millville to journey down to Bivalve. The later afternoon can provide unusual opportunities for marine photographs and scenes that will make the artist reach for brushes and paint.

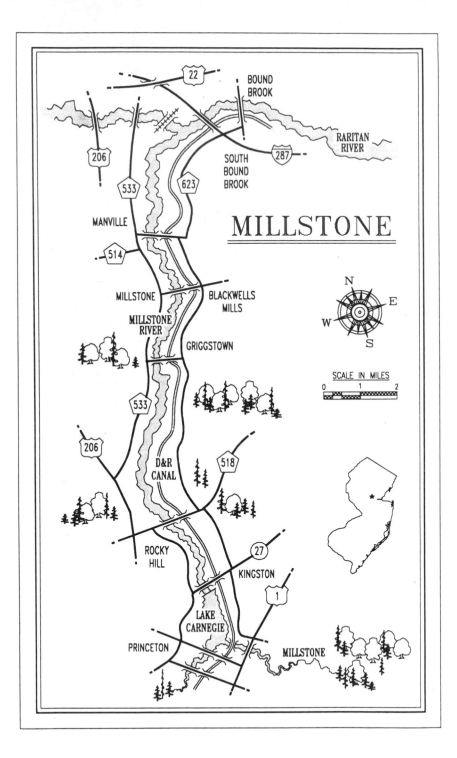

The Millstone

Mattawong was the name the people native to the area gave to this river, and it meant "hard to travel." Conditions must have changed considerably since the early days, as we know of no other stream in the state that is so placid and so easy to negotiate.

Of the many little streams throughout the state the Millstone is one of the most attractive and picturesque. From Kingston to the mouth of the river near Bound Brook it is a quiet-flowing stream, bordered with pleasant meadows and woods.

The origin of the name of the river—which may have once been called "Milestone," or named for a place in Scotland—is unclear. The early settlers did build a number of gristmills along its banks. The dams and many of the early tailraces are intact, but except for the mill at Kingston none of the mill buildings still stand. The most notable characteristic of the river, particularly between Kingston and Griggstown, is the canopy of river birch trees overhead.

Like so many of the smaller streams of the state, the Millstone is fed by more than one branch. One branch is the outlet of a swampy pond near Manalapan on Route 33; the other starts near Hightstown, not far away.

Winding their tortuous ways through swampland and woods and at times twisting back upon the original course in long, sluggish loops, the two branches meet a few miles east of Princeton. A riot of vegetation lines the shores for miles, and the very nature of the country provides a perfect bird sanctuary. Wild ducks, bittern, heron, and many other species of birds may be found in abundance. The color of the autumn leaves along the Millstone is marvelous to see.

Canoeists should start their trip downriver at Scudders Mills monument on Kingston Road, where the river meets Lake Carnegie. It is a simple matter to provide oneself with the transportation facilities for a canoe journey of a few hours, a day, or even a weekend if the objective is to cruise the entire river.

The Scudders Mills monument marks the place where an aqueduct, built in the 1830s, carries the Delaware and Raritan Canal over the river. The canoeist will of course have to carry up and over the canal and into Lake Carnegie at this point. The generosity of the late Andrew Carnegie made possible this delightful man-made lake, which not only adds to the beauty of the countryside but also provides a place for rowing, canoeing, and other aquatic

Footbridge across the Delaware and Raritan Canal at Lake Carnegie. The canal originally crossed the Millstone in an aqueduct well above the river. When Lake Carnegie was created, the Millstone at this point was raised to the level of the canal.

The Princeton University boathouse on Lake Carnegie.

sports for Princeton University and the community of Princeton. It was built in 1906 through the simple expedient of constructing a dam across a natural valley between the Princeton University campus and the Delaware and Raritan Canal. The lake is about three miles long and perhaps a quarter of a mile wide, flanked on the east by the canal towpath and on the west by the winding, wooded shores on the outskirts of Princeton.

At the upper end of the lake, on the west shore, stands the commodious boathouse in which the shells of the university are kept. Such famed events as the Childs Cup Race are held on the lake in the spring. The popularity of dinghy racing has come to Princeton, and there is quite a large fleet of sailing dinghies moored near the lower end, where the lake is wider and the breezes are steadier. When cold weather comes, Lake Carnegie is popular with skaters and skate sailors, who may be seen skimming over its smooth surface during the winter weekends.

Stony Brook (see "Small Streams") empties into the south end of the lake and helps to provide a constant supply of water. Some

The stone bridge over the Millstone River at Kingston. This bridge was built in 1798, replacing an earlier one destroyed during the Revolutionary War. The mill, the bridge, and the surrounding area between the river and the canal are preserved as a small state park.

Rockingham, Washington's headquarters on Route 518 at Rocky Hill.

of the land along the west shore of Lake Carnegie is privately owned, and picnicking there is not allowed. However, across the lake anywhere on the canal towpath picnicking is permitted, and parking is available at many of the bridge crossings in the Delaware and Raritan Canal State Park.

Below the dam on Lake Carnegie the river again assumes its natural form, and this part of the stream to the mill dam, a hundred yards below, is good bass-fishing water. It is here also that a great variety of bird life may be seen, including flocks of Canada geese during the fall and spring months. It is a great thrill to hear them honking and to see them swinging down in the typical large flying V.

The Millstone River is interesting not only from a scenic point of view but in many other respects. According to geologists, it originally flowed in the opposite direction, and during the Ice Age its course reversed. Its original source was a huge spring in the Sourland Mountains, from which it flowed south to empty into the Delaware River near Trenton. It now flows north and empties

A bit of fast water downstream from the bridge at Rocky Hill—a good place to stop for lunch.

the state, with the assistance of the Rockingham Association. It is open to the public; there is a small admission charge.

Although the Millstone traverses the north central section of New Jersey between New York and Philadelphia, the countryside visible from the river remains today much as it was one hundred years ago. Commercial activities along the river have actually decreased during that time.

Following the course of the river from Princeton to Bound Brook runs the historic Delaware and Raritan Canal, to which a full chapter in this volume is devoted. At some places the river runs within a dozen feet of the canal, and at others they are a few hundred feet apart.

At Griggstown the tailrace from the river turned the wheel of a gristmill that operated for many years. Only the foundations of that mill are left, and a modern house has been built on them. Here also, the house occupied by John Honeyman during the Revolution can be seen from the river. Legend has it that Honeyman was Washington's personal spy and that he supplied the information about the strength of the British in Trenton that enabled Washington to make the historic crossing of the Delaware on Christmas night in 1776.

Griggstown, like the other once-busy little canal ports in the valley, still retains its charm. Many of the early houses have been restored. Meadows unfold between the river and the canal along this stretch of water, continuing downriver past the old iron bridge. The Delaware and Raritan Canal State Park provides an access point to the river, along with parking, restrooms, and a canal museum. In this area the yellow cow lilies, or candocs as they are known locally, are most noticeable. They line the banks for miles, and the light green of their leaves makes a colorful contrast to the yellow flowers.

At Blackwell's Mills the milldam is easily negotiated. The mill is long gone, but the miller's house still stands across the road. The Blackwell's Mills Delaware and Raritan Canal State Park access area is here, along with an 1835 canal house that is within walking distance of the river. Soon the canoeist will reach the west-shore location of the Van Doren house. Here Washington and his staff were quartered overnight during their retirement through the valley after the Battle of Princeton.

INDIAN MILL STONE
A REMNANT OF THE
FIRST
AMERICAN MECHANIC
PRESENTED TO JR.O.U.A.M.
NO. 110 BY GEO. GARRETSON

Referred to on the plaque as an Indian millstone, this mortar, now in front of the Old
Forge Museum, was found nearby at the site of
an Indian village.

A short distance downstream is the village of Millstone, originally called Somerset Court House, and one should plan to spend an hour or so here. The restored blacksmith shop contains a large collection of tools and mechanical equipment spanning two hundred years and an anvil believed to have been brought from Holland in the 1600s. The shop is known to have been in operation from 1768 to 1959, and it is probably much older than its first authenticated date would indicate. An antique shop, a gift shop, and other stores are nearby.

In the churchyard of the Dutch Reformed Church on River Road at Millstone are the graves of some of the early settlers. Nearby, a marker commemorates the courthouse of Somerset County that was burned by Simcoe's Raiders in the Revolution. The Indian mortar at the forge was found on the Van Doren farm, which is on the site of a large Indian village.

At Weston, a pre-Revolution gristmill stood until destroyed by flood a number of years ago; the foundation is still there. In 1777, a party of British foragers was defeated here in "the skirmish at Weston Mill" by several hundred militiamen under General Dickenson.

From Weston to the Raritan River, where it ends, the Millstone is too shallow for easy paddling, and because of industrial activity and pollution, it is not desirable for canoeing.

The Mullica

Copper-hued faces, topped by feathered headdresses, are no longer seen among the trees on the shores of the Mullica, and yet it would seem perfectly natural to find Indians still roaming through the area. Near here, on the earliest Indian reservations established in 1758, the last of the New Jersey Indians lived. In 1801 they sold their land and moved to the Oneida Indian Reservation in northern New York State. One member of the tribe, known as Indian Ann, remained on the reservation in New Jersey and lived to be more than a hundred years old.

Atsion, originally called Atsayunk, was named for a local tribe of Indians. Another group adopted the name of Mullica and so honored their friend and patron, Eric Mullica, who settled his Swedish colony on the shores of the river in 1697.

The Mullica was one of the shore rivers to which Indians from as far away as Minisink Island on the upper Delaware River made annual visits to feast on the oysters for which the river was famed. Today, in places along the shores and on some of the islands, heaps of shells remain as evidence of those early visits.

As one paddles quietly down the upper reaches of the river, the journey is through wild forest lands. From Highway 206 all the way to Sweetwater the stream is within the Wharton State Forest. There are no buildings or settlements along the way. The spiritual presence of the original inhabitants seems somehow to pervade the whole area.

Unlike most other Pine Barrens waterways, the Mullica cannot be easily explored by car, as only sand roads parallel both sides of it from its source down to tidewater. The only parts of the river

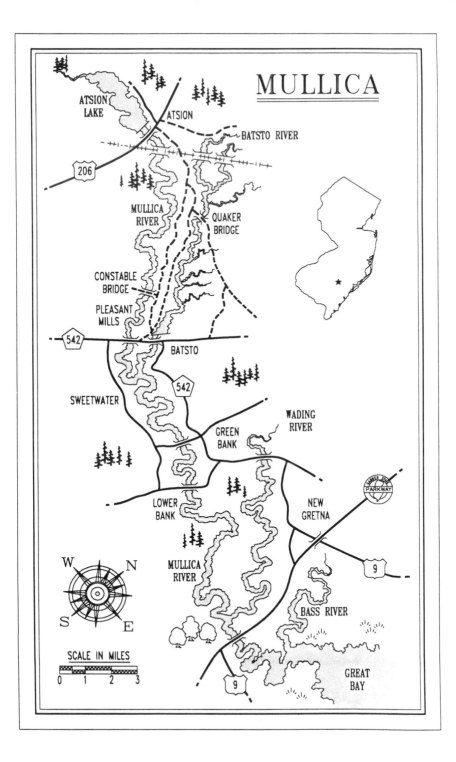

that can be safely explored by car are the area along the north shore of Atsion Lake and the area below Sweetwater, where modern roads permit following the river to the ocean.

For those who have the experience and stamina, a good starting place is just below Atsion Lake and Route 206. At that point the river is narrow and fast and, years ago, was sometimes blocked by brush and fallen trees. Today the river is cleared regularly and maintained for canoeing. Once having begun a trip, however, there is no return except on foot along a sand road (easy to find in some places and difficult in others). The Atsion Lake starting point calls for five or six hours of paddling to reach a take-out point just below the Route 542 bridge at Batsto. Chances are good that you will encounter a beaver dam on the first half of your trip, although its exact location is entirely up to the beavers.

The less experienced or anyone preferring an easier cruise should plan to start at Constable Bridge. From there to Batsto is only a few hours' paddle, allowing plenty of time for some pickerel fishing and lunch on the way down. If you have a four-wheel-drive vehicle, it is possible to drive to Constable Bridge. Otherwise,

| *Negotiating a bend near Atsion.*

| *Running a beaver dam—nice work if you can get it.*

it may prove less expensive to have one of the canoe-rental proprietors drive you and your canoe there. There are several good canoe rentals along the lower Mullica. The proprietors know the river and conditions, and with their six- or eight-canoe trailers can supply as many canoes as may be needed. Perhaps some day the local sand roads will be surfaced, but we hope not, as that would spoil the clean wilderness it is possible to enjoy now.

For those of you who have never negotiated one of the Pine Barrens sand roads or worse yet had your axle buried in the powdery sand, we urge you not to try it. We make it a practice, before trying to take our two-wheel-drive car over any unfamiliar sand road, to look up the park rangers at Batsto Village and ask them if it is possible. If they advise against trying it, take their advice. The Forest Service prohibits travel along some of the sand roads.

During the spring, when there is plenty of water, it is possible to float down the river. One has to keep alert, however, as the fast current sweeping around the bends, sometimes under overhanging brush or fallen timber, can be disastrous or can at least cause one to split a paddle. On this trip an extra paddle or two may be good insurance. A small camp saw or axe may prove helpful in some places, since trees can fall into the river at any time, as the banks are constantly being eroded.

As would be expected, this wild paradise is full of many kinds of game. Deer, grouse, and quail are plentiful. According to hunters and local game officials, the wild turkey is now staging a comeback. So now we have once again both the cranberries and the wild turkey as they were before the advent of the white man.

On a cruise of the Mullica in early May, the profusion of wild plants and flowers was a delight. That rare water plant, the golden club, was well above the surface of the river, and the intriguing fiddleheads of ferns could be seen everywhere along the banks. The pure white seashore sand, sometimes to a height of three to ten feet above the river, was in vivid contrast to the green of the pine and cedar forest above, reminding us that much of New Jersey was under the ocean at one time.

As we paddled along during that spring cruise, we agreed that sometime, perhaps in October, we would again cruise the Mullica but make it a two-day trip camping overnight on one of those delightful sandy shores. (One needs to make camping reservations well in advance at the ranger station at Atsion Lake or at Batsto Village.)

The site of the community of Pleasant Mills was a favorite haunt of the Lenape. There is a lake of some size they knew as Nescochague. On its shores stands an imposing manor house, built in 1754.

A great deal of interest and romance dating back to the eighteenth century surrounds the manor. The owner's daughter, Honoria Reid, is said to have been the heroine of Peterson's novel *Kate Aylesford*, which dealt with the historic background of this area. The novel enjoyed wide popularity many years ago. It told of the adventures of Kate, who was seized by the notorious Pine Barrens robber Joe Mulliner and held for ransom. She was eventually rescued by local citizens led by a British officer—whom she later married, of course. The exploits of Mulliner and his gang of "refugees," as they styled themselves, are still being talked about in this region. We were regaled with several of these yarns by the proprietor of the Sweetwater Casino on the river while lunching

A tranquil place to rest, have lunch, and explore.

there some years ago. It is said that some of the local people regarded this outlaw as a modern Robin Hood. To the majority, however, he was just a bandit.

Joe and his gang operated along the shores of the Mullica for many years, during which his depredations ranged from petty thievery to large-scale robbery. We were told how his many successes led to greater boldness and how, despite the price on his head, he began to appear at dances and other social functions. On one such occasion a special reception was planned for him by a group of outraged citizenry, with the result that on a summer evening in 1781 the bold bandit was captured and hanged from a nearby tree.

The Mullica River played a dramatic part in the Revolutionary War. Pleasant Mills was at that time an important industrial center. In fact, during the blockade of New York and Philadelphia by the British, the nearby Batsto forges and furnaces were the chief source of cannonballs for the Continental Army.

Near Batsto the river is wider and canoes can move along swiftly—if the paddlers still have the energy.

When the British realized their blockade was not a success, they decided to send gunboats up the Mullica, destroy the fleet of American privateers on the way, and then burn the Batsto works. In the ensuing engagement between the British and American fleets, the British not only were attacked by the American sea forces but were hammered by the cannons of the militia from the shore. It was evident the British plans would not succeed.

Having been whipped at what has since been known as the Battle of Chestnut Neck, the British did not again attempt to take the Batsto works. Batsto continued to supply the Continental forces with ammunition throughout the Revolutionary War.

The broad reaches of the lower Mullica and the plentiful supply of pine and oak were a natural combination for the development of the shipbuilding industry in the early nineteenth century. Shipyards lined both shores all the way to Great Bay, and in them were built some of the famous clipper ships.

For its last twelve miles, this river is decidedly not for cruising in a canoe unless one is accustomed to the vagaries of wind-swept salt water. It is delightful sailing or powerboat water, and special boat trips are arranged for parties who want to see the river or stop in at one of the marinas or restaurants along the way.

The Musconetcong

$\mathcal{E}$xcept for early spring and periods following heavy rain, the Musconetcong is difficult to explore by canoe. Nevertheless, we consider it one of the most interesting rivers in New Jersey, with the wooded hills through which it passes and the few remnants of the old 102-mile-long Morris Canal. The canal, along with its thirty-four locks and twenty-three inclined planes, is now practically gone, but for many years during the nineteenth century it was the chief means of conveying coal, iron, and zinc across the northern part of the state to the Hudson River at Jersey City.

The river is the outlet of Lake Musconetcong, and both the river and the lake were principal sources of water to keep the Morris Canal filled. Therefore, any story of the river would be incomplete if it did not include the story of the canal.

Until a few decades ago, it was possible to paddle a canoe on the canal from Stanhope west almost to Waterloo. Now most of it has been filled in through Stanhope and beyond. One of the streets of Stanhope bears the name Plane Street and is a reminder that at one time an inclined plane for lifting the canal barges was located there.

The river, which runs beside the canal from the lake, crosses over the canal at this point and continues as a small stream to Waterloo, four miles to the west. It is possible to make the canal journey on foot along the towpath. Smaller planes, plane houses, and other structures used on the canal will be seen along the way.

From either Stanhope or Netcong, Route 604, which runs along much of the river, will take you to Waterloo Village. Water-

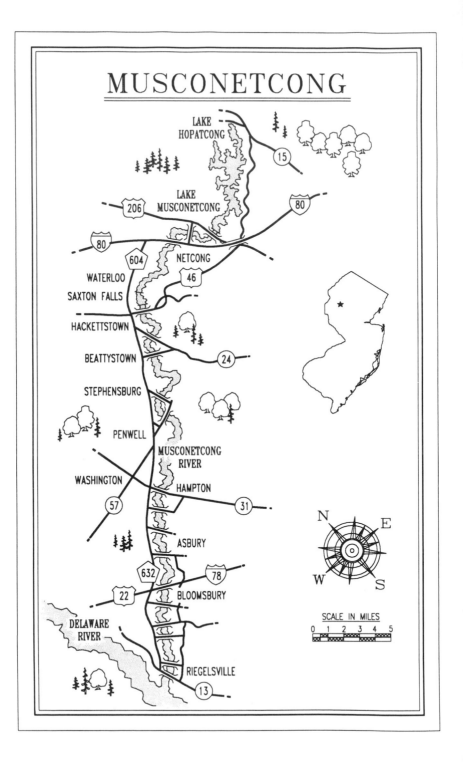

The north shore of Lake Musconetcong looking east from Route 206. The lake is the head-waters of the Musconetcong River.

loo, an eighteenth-century village that prospered from early iron-mining and later from the operation of the Morris Canal, very nearly became a ghost town in the hills. About thirty years ago, however, it was decided that the one-time charm and beauty of the historic landmark should be restored. As a result of the efforts and money spent on the restoration the village appears today little changed from its earlier days and annually attracts thousands of visitors to see and enjoy the old storehouse and country store on the bank of the canal, the blacksmith shop, the old church, and the many other restored buildings now open to the public. Nearby, a replica of a Lenape village has recently been added. Excellent musical programs and crafts shows are a part of the summer activities, but, unfortunately, canoeing is not allowed within the village complex.

Waterloo was founded by Peter Louis Smith, and for many years it was the terminus of the Sussex Railroad of New Jersey.

The Waterloo storehouse from which local farm products were loaded onto canal barges for shipment on the Morris Canal. It is a part of the restoration of this interesting eighteenth-century village. On the first floor is the old general store.

The railroad was built to carry zinc from Franklin Furnace and iron from Andover. They were loaded onto the canal boats and then transported to Newark and Jersey City by canal.

The intact part of the canal that extends south from Waterloo toward Saxton Falls offers an opportunity for walks along the old towpath, and one wouldn't be surprised to see a canal barge towed by mules come around the bend.

Below Waterloo we find the river running beside the canal again, and at this point it widens out into more of a stream. However, there is seldom water enough to permit canoeing except during the spring floods. Hundreds of fishways and dams offer too many obstructions for easy cruising during normal height of water. These man-made devices have been installed throughout the entire river, particularly in the stretch from Waterloo to Hackettstown, to provide good fishing waters. Probably more work has been done for fish propagation on this stream than on any other

Trout fishing is excellent in this part of the river, and the stream is heavily stocked in season. Good luck and perhaps some skill on opening day may give you a catch like this one, and then again perhaps not.

in the state. We commend this stream to the disciples of Isaak Walton, who said:

I care not, I, to fish in seas—
Fresh rivers best my mind do please,
Whose sweet calm course I contemplate,
And seek in life to imitate.

A few miles below Waterloo is Saxton Falls, where the river has been dammed since the time of the building of the canal. Control gates and locks may be seen near the dam. The lake is a beautiful area of water, and one may paddle a canoe upstream for a mile or so. This is a favorite spot with trout fishermen, and the state has provided tables and fireplaces for their enjoyment. A short distance below, at Stephens State Park, very attractive

The pool below Saxton Falls is annually the subject of statewide press coverage on the opening day of trout fishing. Usually a photograph is featured showing fishermen shoulder to shoulder around the pool.

stretches of water and all necessary facilities for a day beside the river can be found.

For many years, the State Fish Hatchery in Hackettstown was open to the public. This hatchery is still active, but tours are now given only at the Pequest hatchery, which is located off Route 46 about ten miles west of Hackettstown. Trout, bass, and other fish are raised at both locations to supply the lakes and streams of New Jersey. Some of the trout one may see in the pools are so large they seem unreal. Thirty-six-inch fish are not at all unusual—and that seems like a lot of fish to an angler who is accustomed to taking one or two ten-inch fish from the streams during the season.

Continuing on Routes 57 and 632 along the river toward Washington, you will pass through Beattystown, which was a settlement before the Revolution. A few miles below Stephensburg, at Penwell, is a very interesting arched stone bridge with an intricate fishway below it.

Most canoe trips on the Musconetcong start between Hackettstown and Stephensburg and continue down to either Hamp-

A picturesque section of the river in Stephens State Park.

ton or Asbury. It is best to do this section during high water in the spring, before trout season opens. Another chance is often afforded in early November, when the dam at Lake Hopatcong State Park is opened to drop the water level of Lake Hopatcong to enable dock repair. There are sometimes opportunities during the summer after several days of rain, but care should be taken during high water because dams, low bridges, and strainers along the shore can make for very dangerous conditions.

Many old canal towns—Washington, Stewartsville, Port Colden, and others—remind one in many ways of the early canal days. Old-timers still tell tall tales that have somehow grown with the years. At Port Colden the route of the canal was directly west to the Delaware at Phillipsburg. One may still see the remains of the canal banks here and there along the road.

At Asbury the Musconetcong develops a lakelike character because of the dam under Route 643. Asbury is one of those exceedingly lovely little villages so common to North Jersey. It consists of a few dozen houses, a grocery store, the usual white country churches, and one industrial plant, a graphite factory. We love this little village and the rolling countryside surrounding it, and we have enjoyed many happy hours here during the bird-shooting season in November.

Below Asbury the river is also quite picturesque, but there is no road near enough to permit one to enjoy much of it by car until Bloomsbury is reached. The mile or so of the Musconetcong as it passes through that village is very attractive, and because of the additional depth of water backed up by a new dam, it is used extensively for boating and fishing. Bloomsbury dates back to the stagecoach days when the present Route 22 was the old Easton Pike. In the village and surrounding countryside are many of the old and substantial stone houses of that earlier day.

From Warren Glen, a paper-making community, the road runs beside the river all the way to the Delaware. Along the road are many old houses and a few of the early settlements—once busy places but now off the beaten track. The whole scene appears as something from the past, and many beautiful views unfold before the traveler as the river is followed. Photographers will be delighted with the subjects they find as the Delaware, and the end of our little river, is reached.

The Oswego
River and Lake

During our explorations seeking material and photographs for the first edition of this book, which was published in 1942, we were familiar with the Wading River from Chatsworth to tidewater. The story of the river's wildness and the unbelievable tangle of fallen timber we had to cut our way through was fully recounted at that time. A few years later we were invited by our good friends Mr. and Mrs. Malcolm Runyon to cruise what was then known as the Oswego Branch of the Wading River. We thus became familiar with this lovely stream with its shores covered with heavy stands of white cedar. After that first cruise we paddled down from Oswego Lake to Harrisville many times, and it became our favorite canoeing water.

The source of the river lies above present-day Oswego Lake, a beautiful area of water extending over ninety acres. Feeding into it and bordering one shore of the lake flows the Oswego River. The lake is at the edge of the 33,000-acre Penn State Forest. Before the present causeway was built to create the larger and deeper lake, it was a cranberry bog.

The lake and the swimming and picnicking facilities offer an opportunity to enjoy both a day of exploration and a swim afterward. If an overnight camp is planned, followed by a day of paddling down the river to Harrisville—a four-hour cruise—one may camp at the state campgrounds at either Bodine Field near Harrisville or at Godfrey Bridge off Route 563 near Jenkins. Both areas are part of the Wharton State Forest. A camping permit may be obtained from Batsto State Park headquarters.

If you view with despair the ever-increasing pollution of our

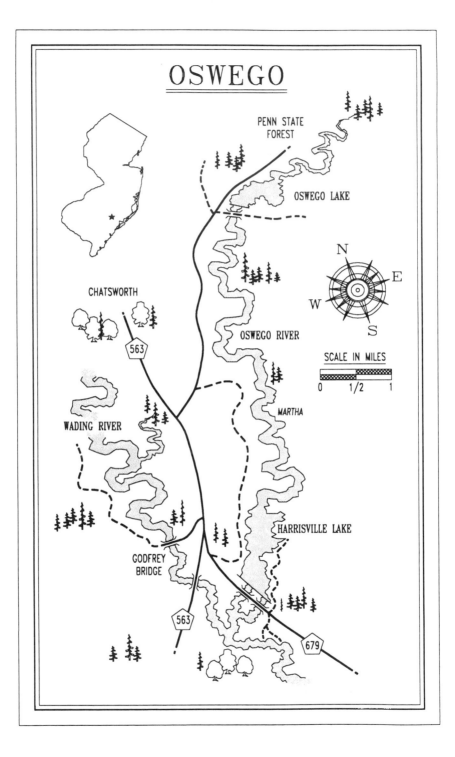

A view of Oswego Lake, the starting point for a trip down to Oswego.

air and water, and the despoliation of our land, not to mention the almost total absence of clean water, take a day off, preferably a weekday, pick up a canoe from some rental place on the way, and drive down to Penn State Forest, the wildest and most beautiful area of Burlington County, in the Pine Barrens.

Walk along the sandy shores of the lake and enjoy a rare sight—water so clean that every pebble and grain of sand is clearly visible. Farther out in the lake, where the water is deeper, it is a beautiful amber color from the cedar roots on the lake bottom. Believe it if you can, the entire lake is *clean* water, and some people claim that it is actually potable.

After a leisurely paddle around the perimeter of the lake, enjoy a picnic lunch and perhaps a refreshing swim in the lake. Following lunch carry your canoe over the causeway below the lower end of the lake and start the cruise from that point to Harrisville. The beauty and wildness of the Oswego River on this journey through the Wharton State Forest cannot be matched in many of the wilderness areas of America.

If you are fortunate enough to have one of the usual fine spring or fall days, you will breathe clean air for a change and see the unbelievable wildness and beauty of the river and the wild-flowers, said to include at least twenty-five species not found any-where else on earth. At the end of a day on the stream you will regretfully leave the river for the journey home.

Due to the fact that all of Lake Oswego and most of the river are within the Penn and Wharton State forests, they will, we hope, remain forever in their wild state. In our opinion, unless every one of us begins to do more about our environmental spoil-age than just talk, view with alarm, and hold rallies, it is very likely that one day not too far into the future the Pine Barrens may be the only area in New Jersey where we shall be able to breathe *clean* air and see *clean* water and unspoiled wilderness.

If there is any doubt in your mind about the necessity of pre-serving this great heritage, the Pine Barrens, we suggest a careful

Not numbered among the rare wildflowers and water plants of the Pine Barrens, fiddle-head ferns grow in profusion along the Os-wego. During early May these intriguing plants appear exactly like the head of a fiddle.

Beaver activity above Martha on the Oswego River. The beaver are making a comeback in this part of the Pine Barrens.

reading of an interesting and informative booklet that may be obtained without charge from the Division of Parks and Forestry in Trenton or at any state park in New Jersey. It is entitled *The Pine Barrens of New Jersey*.

Most canoeing groups make the run from the lake to Harrisville in half a day, as camping is not permitted along the river. Groups of Scouts camp at Bodine Field just below the Harrisville dam.

When camping in this area, we reduce the risk of an uncontrolled brush fire by cooking our meals on a single-burner stove and dispensing with evening campfires.

About three-quarters of the way down, the river opens into a pondlike area with many submerged cedar stumps. This is the remnant of Martha Pond, which provided water power to operate the iron forge at Martha. At the end of the pond the stream flows through an opening in what appears to be a large, man-made concrete structure. It isn't, however. It is actually a dam that is composed of the hard core of a deposit of bog iron that used to be mined in the vicinity, before the discovery of the harder ores of Pennsylvania. It is the only such natural dam we know of. Several prominent geologists with whom we have discussed this agree that it must be a natural dam. There was no reason for ever building a dam in that area, even during the days of bog-iron smelting.

The forests of southern Atlantic white cedar, with the sharp treetops outlined against the sky, the amber-colored sweet water, and the thrill of seeing an osprey frantically trying to gain altitude as you paddle around a bend, are all sights and experiences you will long remember. Incidentally, the cedars in the area are said to be unequaled in size and quantity anywhere else in northeastern America.

The tree roots, where they are above the surface of the swamp

Ruins of the paper mill on the river at Harrisville. The mill was at one time the center of the prosperous community and like so many of the Pine Barrens enterprises died as a result of technological progress. The walls of the mill were of stone and three feet thick.

Harrisville Lake, located on Route 563, the termination point for a trip down the Oswego.

water and the moist ground, are covered with sphagnum moss. The dense shade of the forested areas provides an ideal environment for rare ferns and shade-tolerant wildflowers.

The Oswego is becoming more popular each year with outing groups, canoe clubs, and Scout groups. While it is doubtless a fact that more and more people enjoy the wilderness cruise down the river, it never seems crowded. The many bends and the forests crowding down close to the water quickly lose one group as another takes off, and thus, while there may be a hundred canoes on the river at the same time, they are strung out for several miles.

It may seem strange that in this very populous state, should one wreck a canoe on the upper part of this river, it would be difficult if not impossible to get through the tangled swamp and forest to a highway. There is little chance of such an event, however, in this day of sturdy aluminum and plastic canoes, but an upset can occur if one doesn't carefully watch for the logs and roots. Such a spill could be unfortunate, as it was to one couple who did turn over in the water on a cold October day. The dunking they got was not only uncomfortable, but the upset cost them a hundred dollars to replace a special camera lens they lost.

The most enjoyable and comfortable times to cruise in this area are during May and June and late September and October. At other times it is usually hot and buggy or too cold and raw to be thoroughly enjoyed.

The Passaic

This slow-moving, roving stream, the second largest river in New Jersey, has its source in the Bernardsville Mountains. The Passaic is hardly a brook as it flows through the Jockey Hollow section of Morristown National Historical Park. It can be observed as it tumbles alongside Hardscrabble Road in Bernardsville and again behind the Old Mill Inn. A dam at Madisonville Road forms Osborn Pond. From its headwaters to Newark Bay, into which it drains, the Passaic is over eighty-five miles long and passes through or borders seven counties. It is a river of great diversity of terrain and is subject to flood conditions, which often cause it to leave the normal channels and spread over the adjoining countryside for miles.

The Wisconsin Ice Sheet, the last glacier to cover the northern part of the state, reached the Paterson–Little Falls area on its way south about 15,000 years ago. Several thousand years later it had advanced to its southern terminus at what is now Basking Ridge. For many thousands of years, the valley of the Passaic from Paterson to Moggy Hollow was filled with ice several thousand feet in depth.

When the ice began to melt and the glacier to recede, Lake Passaic was formed. It was a body of water over thirty miles long and from eight to twelve miles wide. Before the erosion through Moggy Hollow and what is now the Millington Ravine began, the lake was in places nearly two hundred feet deep.

An interesting geologic fact about the glacier that created the ancient lake is that in its retreat the gap in the first Watchung

PASSAIC

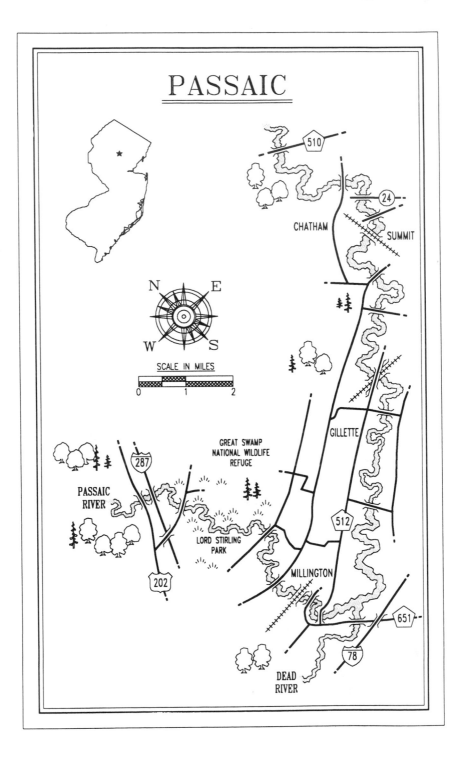

Mountain at what is now Short Hills was sealed with debris, changing the course of the Hudson River, which had previously flowed through it. Over a long period of time the lake gradually drained away, primarily through Moggy Hollow near Liberty Corner, and through the Millington Ravine to the present channel of the Passaic River.

Today the actual remnants of that ancient lake may be seen at three places along the Passaic River. They are the Great Swamp (a national wildlife refuge near Basking Ridge), the Hatfield Swamp at Hanover, and the Great Piece Meadows farther downstream. Those swamps are the only evidence that remains today of that once-great body of glacial melt known as Lake Passaic.

In the course of a single day of exploration on this river, one observes mile after mile of farmlands being developed into houses and condominiums; and then, without warning, areas of swampland and marshes close in on the stream. It becomes a modern wilderness in the midst of densely populated North Jersey. Deer are plentiful, and in 1990 a bear was captured in Summit and removed to a less populated area of the state. Wild ducks and Canada geese use the Passaic and its marshes to rest on their long migrations north and south, and some geese are year-round residents. Great blue herons and green herons reside in the area. In the swamps and marshes a total of one hundred different species of birds have been seen and identified in a single day.

During the spring, and after a rain, it is possible to paddle a canoe on any part of the river. Even in the driest weather, one can launch a canoe at the Somerset County Environmental Education Center access and paddle into the Great Swamp. Draining the swamp are Black Brook and Great Brook, and these rivulets offer hours of exploration for birdwatching. This is also a good spot to start a downriver paddle. From this point, one may paddle all the way to Singac.

The river flows in a southeasterly direction through the Great Swamp, then breaks through a range of hills at Basking Ridge and hurries through a mile-long ravine to strike the valley at Millington. The early settlers took full advantage of this fast water and built their gristmills below the ravine. Shallow water in the gorge is the rule until the Route 512 bridge is reached, but below that

View of the Great Swamp, remnant of ancient Lake Passaic, from the Passaic River put-in on Lord Stirling Road in Basking Ridge.

Some Monoco Canoe Club members taking advantage of the drainage ditch on Lord Stirling Road to gain access to the Passaic at high water.

point there is plenty of water for cruising in all but the driest seasons. Along both shores is the typical meadowland with plenty of oak forest near the river.

At Summit there is a small dam, but it is easily portaged on the right. Here Union County has developed a small park with picnic tables, which makes a nice spot for lunch.

Some idea of the manner in which the Passaic wanders in its course may be realized from the fact that while one may drive from Millington to Summit in a few minutes, it takes a full day of paddling to reach the same point by canoe. The river loops and turns continuously and in fact flows in every direction somewhere during its journey. It is pleasant canoeing water, as few settlements intrude upon it until Chatham is reached. A great deal of canoeing is done on this part of the Passaic.

For many years, beyond the memory of the oldest inhabitants of the Passaic valley, disastrous floods have each spring swept down the river and caused millions of dollars' damage to property and sometimes loss of life. The New Jersey Flood Control Commission and the Army Corps of Engineers have tried, with little success to date, to develop some method for controlling the rampaging waters. As the flood waters overflow into the vast expanse of meadowlands, they also bring on a mosquito problem.

Some fifty years ago a plan was considered and widely publicized that was hoped to be the answer to the flood problem. It called for the virtual re-creation of ancient glacial Lake Passaic. It was believed that such a huge man-made lake would check and hold the floodwaters for gradual release downstream. Even at that time, however, before the great increase in housing and industry, the estimated cost was staggering. Today the cost of the land and the building of the reservoir would be astronomical.

Various agencies, county, state, and federal, are making headway in controlling the pollution in the lower river; however, the job is far from completed. For years asbestos was dumped in the Great Swamp and on the bank in Millington. This is high on the list of major cleanups.

While the Passaic is not beautiful in the sense that the Great Egg Harbor, the Rancocas, the Millstone, and other New Jersey rivers are, it has a charm of its own. It is the beauty of the silent and mysterious swampland, and it offers many unusual photo-

According to tradition, in this lovely old church not far from the river a balcony collapsed in 1838, and the village was renamed New Providence in thankfulness that no one was injured. In the 1980s the original steeple was replaced with an exact replica.

Where the river widens, meadows filled with wildflowers reach down to its banks.

The Passaic, with water about three feet higher than normal.

graphic opportunities for those who like to record their journeys on film.

There are usually a few fallen trees in the course of the river to Summit, but beyond that point the river is free of obstructions for the remaining thirty-five miles to Little Falls.

At Pine Brook the Whippany River enters from the left. During the early days of the state this tributary stream was known to the Indians as the Whippanong, and many of them made their homes along its shores. All through this part the Passaic winds and twists to such an extent that four miles of travel by water is necessary to cover a mile by land. The current is so slow that it is hardly noticeable, and one may paddle up- or downstream without much effort.

Following a northerly course for another dozen miles, the river then turns to the east, near Towaco, beyond which the Ramapo River adds its volume of water. From here to Singac the river is much wider and deeper. The surrounding countryside is more settled, and permanent homes and summer camps line the shores. The sport of canoeing was in its glory on this part of the stream years ago, and there were literally thousands of privately owned and rental canoes to be seen on any Saturday or Sunday. This local canoeing was quite different from that of the typical cruiser. It was the weekend, radio-blaring, lazy-paddling sort of thing.

A mile below Singac is Little Falls and the end of practical canoeing on this river. High natural falls hemmed in with industrial plants make the portages extremely difficult, and this section should not be attempted. The Morris Canal crossed here on a high, arched aqueduct of stone. Nothing remains of it today.

After its drop over these falls and a short run through the gorge below, the Passaic slows its pace again, and from that point to the Great Falls at Paterson it becomes a slow-moving stream of considerable depth in places. The various communities and the county have developed both shores into a continuous park, ending in Paterson's attractive West Side Park. It was below the site of the park, just above the bridge which crosses the river, that John P. Holland launched his first submarine in May 1881. This crude, one-person craft successfully submerged and was propelled both under and on the waters of the Passaic, and it now proudly rests in the Paterson

Museum. In the park stands one of the earliest of the commercially successful submarines as a monument to Holland.

At one time canoeing was very popular with local people. We were told that private canoe clubs were very numerous between Little Falls and Passaic.

Below the river bridge the Great Falls at Paterson tumble over a traprock precipice a hundred feet in height. This is an impressive sight during the spring floods and in winter when the waterfall is a mass of ice.

Paterson and the river passing near it are intimately associated with a historic enterprise that has become symbolic of American industry. In 1791 an organization known as the Society for Establishing Useful Manufactures was formed under the leadership of Alexander Hamilton. Legislation was granted to permit its functioning. A mile-square area was designated, embracing much of

This handmade sheet-metal submarine is the experimental craft invented by John P. Holland and tested in the nearby Passaic River. It is now in the Paterson Museum.

Perhaps because of their potential for water power, the Great Falls at Paterson were the inspiration for Alexander Hamilton's Society for Establishing Useful Manufactures. The textile mills built here were a part of the first organized manufacturing efforts in America.

what is now the city of Paterson, and purchased by the newly organized company. The plans were centered on the water power available in the falls, and a cotton mill was the first venture. Other budding industries were invited to join the group, but, as in so many ambitious plans of this kind, bickering among the organizers soon disrupted the original plans. However, plants were built independently, and the present city of Paterson is the result.

Years ago the lower part of the river was known as one of the most attractive streams in the eastern part of the country. The Jersey sandstone Dutch colonial homes of the early settlers, surrounded by well-kept yards extending down to the shores of the river, made an attractive picture. Boat clubs were numerous, and some of the most famous scullers of another generation were developed on the river. Along the river road between Newark and Rutherford were large estates, similar to many in the Virginia tidewater area.

With the advent of industrial activity, quick to take advantage of the plentiful supply of pure water and the unexcelled shipping facilities to the ports of the world, the charm and beauty of the ancient Passaic disappeared.

Through Kearny, Nutley, and Rutherford, the river has been cleared of old ship hulks and other debris; unfortunately, now it has tires and other refuse in it. However, the schools of Kearny, Rutherford, and other communities use the Passaic River for sculling practice, and in the spring races are held there.

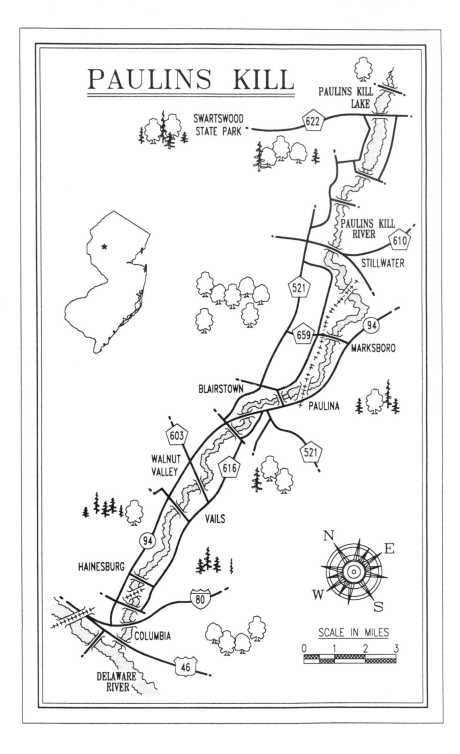

The Paulins Kill

The land through which the Paulins Kill flows presents a bold and picturesque outline. The Kittatinny mountain range parallels the entire course of the river, the rugged hills actually extending to its very shores. The river turns and twists around the many hills as it hurries along to the Delaware. The Lenape named this lovely mountain stream "Tockhockonetkong," and to them the mountains were "Kittatinny" or "chief town," for it was from the shores of the river, protected on the west by the mountain range, that the local chiefs of the Lenape governed their people.

There is an interesting story about the origin of the present name of the stream. Following the Battle of Trenton, some of the Hessian prisoners were taken to the village of Stillwater, and there they were held until the end of the war. Many of them liked the country so much that they bought land and settled permanently. One of them became a prominent man in the affairs of the valley, and the river was named in honor of his daughter, Pauline. Many of the present-day residents of the Paulins Kill valley trace their ancestry back to those Hessian prisoners of war who made this the country of their adoption.

If you look at a map of Sussex and Warren counties, in the extreme northwestern part of the state, you will see how clearly the mountains separate the valley of the Delaware from the Paulins Kill. When viewing these rugged hills from the Delaware Valley, it seems as if some volcanic upheaval must have split the earth along what is now the Delaware River and thus created these two New Jersey counties that form the western barrier to this corner of our state. They rise to an elevation of over 1800 feet at High

Point, and approximately half of their length has been taken over for state parks. We may now enjoy unsurpassed mountain scenery and recreational facilities in the Stokes State Forest and at High Point Park.

The oldest road of any considerable length in the United States follows the east shore of the Delaware. It is the Old Mine Road, built by the Dutch in the seventeenth century, from Kingston, New York, to the Indian copper mines at Pahaquarry, just north of Columbia. Copper was transported by oxcart to Kingston and then shipped to Holland. Much of the road remains today. In fact, it is possible to drive or walk from Columbia to a point near Port Jervis over the ancient road. Beyond that place it becomes lost in the network of modern highways. Had the proposed Tocks Island Reservoir been built, all of the Old Mine Road from the dam site just above the Delaware Water Gap to Port Jervis would have been under water. Happily, the project has been stopped and appears no longer to be a threat.

Springhouses, built over cold springs to keep milk and meat cool, are becoming rare in the New Jersey countryside. This one, built of native sandstone in the mid-eighteenth century, is near Augusta.

Let us climb our rugged Kittatinnies again and go back to the valley of the Paulins Kill. The actual beginning of this river is at a point near Augusta, and for the first few miles it is not much more than a mountain brook. A mile or so farther on, the water is backed up by an old dam, and from there the stream cascades from rock to rock in its quick passage through the many little ravines. The wildest scenery and the fastest water may be found in the few miles from Augusta to the hamlet of Paulins Kill. A few miles below Halsey the river slows down and for the next five miles becomes Paulins Kill Lake, which is paralleled on both sides by hills and meadows, making it a very attractive boating and fishing area. In early years there was a series of small ponds, each with its wooden dam and gristmill. Today one may spend a pleasant afternoon canoeing and fishing along its shores.

It is difficult to explore the upper part of the river, except for an occasional place accessible from the narrow mountain roads. The canoeist does not find it any easier, as it is not possible to paddle on this part of the stream except during high water, and then the rocks and falls make such a trip inadvisable. In fact, cruising on the Paulins Kill should be confined to the section between Stillwater and Columbia and should be planned for spring, when the runoff from the winter snows provides an extra foot of water. It is possible to paddle on some parts of the river at any time, but higher than normal water is required for a continuous trip.

For those who may want to explore the Paulins Kill by car, we advise driving directly from Newton to the foot of Paulins Kill Lake and then continuing downstream via Middleville, Stillwater, Marksboro, Blairstown, Hainesburg, and Columbia. Good roads follow the entire stream.

Another opportunity to explore the Paulins Kill valley is provided by the recently inaugurated Paulins Kill Valley Trail. This trail stretches twenty-six miles along an abandoned railroad bed near the river from its origin at Sparta to the Columbia dam.

There is glorious scenery throughout the valley, and there are many places of historic interest. At Stillwater, for example, the explorer will find a charming village that was the first settlement in the valley. Casper Shafer, a German immigrant, was one of the earliest of the settlers. He built the first crude gristmill and later added a sawmill here in 1750. The products of these mills were

The mill, with the tailrace from the river in the foreground, as it appears today in the quiet little village of Stillwater.

Even in the rain, opening day of trout season brings out the fishermen at Blairstown and all along this popular fishing stream.

A quiet pastoral scene on the Paulins Kill near Hainesburg.

The water below the bridge at Hainesburg is rock-filled and fast.

Remnants of a mid-March snowstorm along the Paulins Kill.

floated down the river on flatboats to the Delaware and thence to Philadelphia. As the lower valley became settled, a great many power dams were built, and it then became necessary to carry the flour and lumber overland in oxcarts. Only one of these small dams remains between Stillwater and Marksboro.

Some potential hazards punctuate the otherwise placid course of the river between Stillwater and Blairstown. The rapids at Marksboro, the most difficult on the river, should be carefully looked over from the right bank, as they continue for several hundred yards below the bridge. Three small ledges just above Paulina Lake require some caution also. Canoes must be carried around the right side of the dam at Paulina, a barrage about ten feet high.

Blairstown, the "gem of the Paulins Kill," is a pleasantly situated town with homes and businesses clustered around the sides and tops of a series of rolling hills. The well-known Blair Academy is located here. The old tailrace has been made into a park which, together with the little lake above it, provides a very pleasant

Layers of wool clothing, mittens, and a thermos of hot coffee—who would believe it's spring?

retreat for summer days. The stone gristmill on the main street is now the town library, and it is an unusually fine example of stonework. While we were photographing it, a local resident pointed out that it is possible to find practically every letter of the alphabet in the combinations of the various mortar joints between the cut stones.

After the river swings around the bend at Hainesburg, it is flanked on both sides by high cliffs which confine the waters of the stream into a stretch of fast rapids. The mile or so through these hills provides a very enjoyable run for the experienced canoeist during spring high water. Canoeists should look this water over very carefully from the shore before attempting to navigate through the rapids.

Hainesburg as a settlement is not very old, although the stone

The Paulins Kill viaduct just below Hainesburg was one of the largest concrete structures in the world when it was built at the turn of the century. It was the route of the Lackawanna Railroad's "crack" train—the Phoebe Snow. A steep climb to the top is rewarded by spectacular views of the countryside.

gristmill on the south shore was built before the Revolution. On the side of the hill one may see some of the old lime kilns. Below Hainesburg a massive concrete railroad viaduct spans the river. It was built in the late nineteenth century to carry the Lackawanna Railroad but is no longer in use. A short but strenuous climb to the top of the viaduct provides spectacular views of the Kittatinny Ridge and the Delaware Water Gap.

A lake of some size has been created through the building of a huge power dam above Columbia, and most canoe trips should end at this lake. A short distance below the dam the waters of the Paulins Kill empty into the Delaware River. Here, one of the largest covered bridges ever built in eastern America spanned the Delaware River. It was built to carry the lighter traffic of the horse era but it carried heavy motor traffic for years. It was replaced by a modern bridge many years ago. The Old Mine Road begins near the New Jersey end of the present bridge.

At one time Columbia seemed destined to be a busy manufacturing town, as several attempts were made to establish a glass-making center there. The glass forges were built in the middle of the last century, passed from one owner to another, and finally were abandoned. Today the village is quiet and peaceful, an excellent place to spend a restful vacation.

PEQUEST

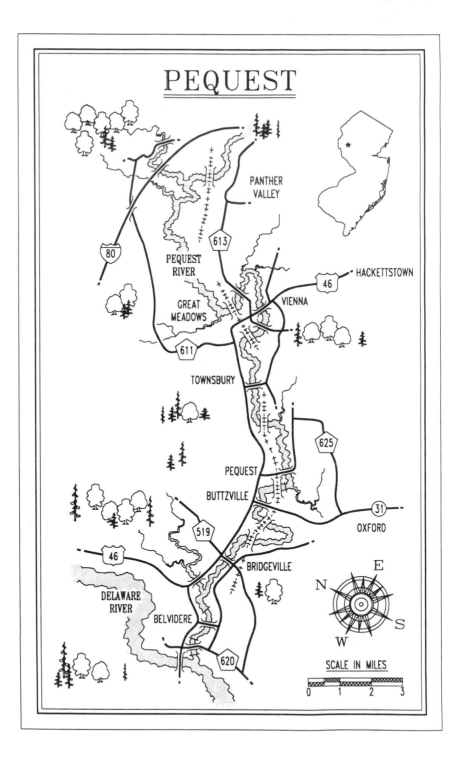

The Pequest

lowing out of the high plains of Sussex County toward the Delaware, the Pequest River is a stream of two characters. From its source in Stickles Pond until it flows through the swampland just underneath Jenny Jump Mountain, the river is a meandering flatlands stream; between Jenny Jump Mountain and Pohatcong Mountain, in the Great Meadows region, the river drains a beautifully rich plain of farmlands. At Townsbury, it starts to tumble toward the Delaware, and this energetic part of the river from Townsbury to Belvidere has become a popular canoeing run.

The Pequest flows out of the northwest corner of Stickles Pond, just at the end of the Newton Airport runway. It remains a little meadow creek as far as the flat expanse of rich farmland in the Great Meadows area between Shades of Death Road (Route 611) and Alphano Road (Route 613). As these roads climb along the rolling boundaries of this land, one can see the dark, rich soil that has produced onions, celery, and lettuce for New Jersey for a century and a half. These farms in Great Meadows, sometimes called "the mucklands," are built on bogland that was drained into the Pequest starting in the 1870s. The high areas in this region are still called "islands," even though they now are only islands from the crops. They used to be islands in a true sense, and they were the site of many Indian camps.

The Pequest flows through a region that is rich with mastodon fossils. We were clued into this when visiting the New Jersey State Museum in Trenton. The larger of the two mastodon skeletons on display there—occasionally called Martha by museum insiders— was found about 1971 on a tributary of the Pequest in Mountain

Lake. Many fossils were exposed in the 1800s when the swampland in Great Meadows was drained. In 1844 there was a record finding of six skeletons—five adults and a calf—grouped as if they were standing together. One from this group found its way to the Museum of Comparative Zoology at Harvard University.

After Great Meadows, the Pequest begins its descent toward the Delaware, and while the river is too low to canoe much of the year, it can be an exciting white-water stream in the spring and after heavy rains. There are many swift spots, and there are at least three points on the river that can be dangerous for canoeists who do not have full control of their boats. Those who are not experienced paddlers should explore the river by car. Route 46 and local streets parallel the lower part of the river.

Make an extra point of caution in the late spring. While the

The education center at the state-operated trout hatchery is open to the public each weekend. This site was chosen for the hatchery because of an abundance of high-quality water that is drawn from a network of eight wells.

Pequest is still canoeable then, it becomes a very popular fishing stream. Canoeists will need to take care during fishing season, since there is likely to be a caster around almost every bend. Indeed, the Pequest is home to the Pequest Trout Hatchery.

The current Pequest Trout Hatchery opened in 1982 and produces over half a million brook, brown, and rainbow trout each year. Not all of these fish are destined for the Pequest. These trout are used to stock hundreds of New Jersey lakes and streams. The whole site of the trout hatchery is within the Pequest Wildlife Management Area, which covers 1500 acres of public land. The hatchery and an adjacent environmental education center are open for general visits every weekend throughout the year and can become quite busy on school days.

The hatchery is fed by a giant aquifer that was found by Frank Markowitz, a state geologist, by watching water disappear in a

A flotilla parked for lunch behind Hot Dog Johnny's on Route 46. This popular stop makes it optional to bring a lunch for the run from Townsbury to Belvidere.

cornfield during a rainstorm. Because the cornfield was on the side of a hill, he expected it to be destroyed by the heavy runoff; however, this did not happen. Upon investigating, Markowitz discovered one of the largest aquifers on the East Coast, capable of supplying the 10,000 gallons of water per minute needed to feed the hatchery. This aquifer was the main reason the state purchased the 1500 acres for the Pequest Wildlife Management Area.

This little stream was one of the favorite fishing spots for President Herbert Hoover. Contemporary scuttlebutt had it that the then-active hatchery would seed the stream with trout just above where the president was casting, making him appear to be quite a successful fisherman. (The old hatchery was about five miles downstream from the current site.)

Canoeists need to pay careful attention to the height of the river. There are many low bridges, and at high water the river can even flow over some of these spans. Perhaps the tightest spot is the footbridge at Island Park, just east of Route 31. Also, the low-head dam near the gauge at Pequest has a dangerous undertow at high water. Therefore, after taking stock of the situation and finding high water—more than three feet on the Pequest gauge—it is strongly recommended that potential canoeists reconsider and head for one of the other local streams. The Musconetcong is just a short distance away and can frequently be run when the Pequest cannot.

At water levels above two feet on the Pequest gauge, you can begin your trip above Townsbury, where the river parallels Route 46. Not far below the put-in is a short, interesting stretch of rapids to the Townsbury bridge. Below the bridge the Pequest meanders through a rock-strewn course where at lower water levels the rocks form a challenging maze. As if running an obstacle course, the Pequest dashes between islands, drops over eel weirs, and follows idyllic channels on its way to the Delaware.

V-shaped ledges seen along the Pequest, especially prevalent near Buttzville and Bridgeville, are the remnants of eel weirs. They were used through the 1940s for trapping eels. Bridgeville is easily identified as the river flows beneath a beautiful eight-arch stone bridge.

Although the canoeist is not always conscious of it, a road runs along the right-hand bank for most of the twelve miles to Belvi-

Remains of an old eel weir.

dere. The tree-lined banks and ravine sometimes provide a sense of remoteness, although civilization is never more than a few hundred feet away.

The Pequest was the source for much industrial advancement in the city of Belvidere. In the 1700s it was diverted from its natural course to a straight run through town. The river was harnessed to power mills, an ice plant, and several factories. Although it is no longer used to generate power, portions of the river still run under some of the town's buildings, and there are two standing dams in town as well. For this reason, canoeists need to take out above town.

Belvidere, the Warren County seat, remains a beautiful Victorian town with many well-maintained structures. It has a long, rich history—the town was known as Greenwich-on-the-Delaware up through 1775—and taking time to explore it on foot would be worthwhile.

The broken dam above Belvidere is the most challenging spot on the Pequest.

The Ramapo–Pompton

The country surrounding the Ramapo River is more rugged than that through which most New Jersey rivers flow. The main branch starts as the outlet of a small pond just east of Route 17, near Tuxedo Park, New York. For several miles it takes on the appearance of a wilderness stream. The majestic forests of Harriman Park form an appropriate background for the river, and in turn the river adds to the beauty of that great recreational park, as the singing waters flow along. There is not sufficient water for cruising above Suffern except during spring floods. In the area of Suffern, much of the stream has lost its original charm because of commercial development.

At times of high water the upper stream sometimes taxes the ability of even the expert canoeist. The high banks confine the full flood, and the boulders and other obstructions create white-water conditions that cause an occasional upset and a swim to shore. For a great many years the members of the Atlantic Division of the American Canoe Association, the sponsor of organized canoeing in America, made an annual event of a spring weekend cruise on this river, starting at Tuxedo.

There is something about such a group cruise that is difficult to describe. The good fellowship of thirty or forty men and women, all keenly interested in the sport; the frequent upsets, rescues, and the sharing of dry clothing; the end of the day and the evening campfire and songs—all are things to be remembered, to be treasured always. It is that indescribable something that has kept the American Canoe Association alive through more than a century. Seventy-year-olds are still active in the affairs of that group.

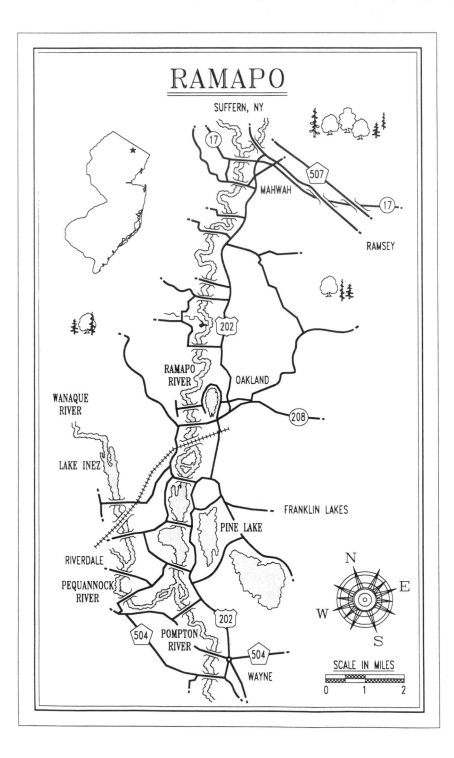

RAMAPO

SUFFERN, NY

MAHWAH

RAMSEY

202

RAMAPO
RIVER

OAKLAND

WANAQUE
RIVER

208

LAKE INEZ

FRANKLIN LAKES

PINE LAKE

RIVERDALE

PEQUANNOCK
RIVER

202

504

POMPTON
RIVER

504

WAYNE

N
E
W
S

SCALE IN MILES

0   1   2

| *The Ramapo began as runoff from the glacier that left these rocks.*

Carrying on the tradition, the Murray Hill Canoe Club and other groups still schedule spring cruises on the Ramapo River. In April 1970, the authors joined the Murray Hill Club for a cruise that was to begin below Mahwah, off Route 202. Upon our arrival at nine o'clock we found some of the members alternately preparing their canoes for the trip and blowing on their hands in the near-freezing temperature.

We had to forgo the pleasure of accompanying the group by canoe. Instead we spent some time photographing the preparations, and after seeing the group disappear around a bend in the river, we had some hot coffee and then followed in our car along Route 202.

At the beginning of the cruise, one of the men, attempting to dodge trees and brush in a bit of fast water, rolled over in the cold water. However, it was a beautiful sunny day, and the canoeist didn't seem to mind his misadventure. Joining the group at their lunch break in the lee of an old bridge, we learned there had been more upsets on the way downstream. By sharing dry clothes with

Part of the fleet of the Murray Hill Canoe Club passing below the high bluff near Darlington.

those who had received a dunking, the group made these incidents seem of little account.

The high enthusiasm of this genial group of people reminded us that in our many years of outdoor activities we have always found canoeists and campers to be happy people, thoroughly enjoying group activities like this cruise. For those interested in such events we suggest joining one of the many canoe clubs that are active throughout New Jersey.

A convenient put-in for this river is at the Ramapo Reservation, located on Route 202 approximately two miles south of Route 17. There is usually adequate parking, and it is a short walk to the river. Other put-ins can be found at various points downriver on side roads off Route 202.

As a part of our photographic coverage of the Ramapo trip we drove downstream looking for a high bluff from which we could get some pictures of the fleet through the trees, on its way downstream. The view from this bluff gives an example of what we were trying to say with our camera, about the thrill of the first canoe trip in the spring when the trees are still bare of foliage and the air is crisp.

Paralleling the river all the way to Pompton Lake, the beautiful and somewhat mysterious Ramapo Mountains loom up. Those

From this bridge, a short walk into Ramapo Reservation leads to an excellent picnic area.

aged hills, where rattlesnakes are said to abound, have always retained their wild and forbidding aspect, and few roads or trails cross them. Some of the people who lived in the fastness of these hills for generations were practically without contact with the modern world. It may seem strange, but until recently there were places in the Ramapo hills where the natives lived in a state comparable to conditions in sections of Appalachia.

All along this stretch of water the huts of Indian tribes once stood. The present village of Oakland was in fact one of the largest of the Indian villages. Today paddlers may encounter deer bounding in and out of the water in front of them, or a couple of heron leading the way. Families of Canada geese are frequently seen along the river.

A mile or so above Oakland the Ramapo enters a valley with the mountains crowding down to the very shores of the stream. Musical little rapids add to the other sounds of nature as the canoeist journeys along. The motorist who drives along Route 202 misses the charm of that part of Oakland which is on the river. From the village downstream to the dam above Pompton Lake the river is very popular with fishermen. It is easy to understand why the Indians loved this spot so much.

Surprisingly, few canoes are seen going down this river. On a recent lovely Sunday morning not one other paddler was passed. This may be due to the recent building of additional dams to prevent flooding, which has stemmed the water flow to a certain extent. This has also made the river more accessible to wading fishermen, and care must be taken to avoid collisions with them or their lines.

During the spring runs some may be tempted to canoe over the low dams encountered on the way. It is a feat that seems easy and perfectly logical to save a carry, but too often it turns out to be a sport for the onlooker alone. Upsets are frequent, and in early April, with the water temperature near freezing, such a mishap could be disastrous. In particular, the dam just below the Ramapo Reservation should be portaged on the left.

Margaret and James Cawley at the Mahwah rendezvous for the start of the Murray Hill Canoe Club cruise in April 1970.

A pleasant vista on the river where it widens out into Pompton Lake above the dam.

The high dam at Pompton where most canoe cruises end.

After leaving the dam below Oakland the river soon begins to widen out into Pompton Lake. For a mile or so the shores are bordered with rushes, and soon one emerges into the lake proper. This lake was built through the damming of the river at the village of Pompton to generate power, but it is as attractive as many of our northern natural lakes. Cottages line both shores, and on the west side are recreational places, boat liveries, and the like. It is also popular in the winter during the skating season. On the high, wooded eastern shore is Sunnybank, the home of Albert Payson Terhune, who was known and loved all over the world for his dog stories. Recent construction of a bridge in this area has somewhat compromised the rustic character.

The lake is quite large, and numerous take-out points can be found along the shores. It is worth a trip by foot or car to the end of the lake to view the impressive dam.

While the present village of Pompton has the appearance of other typical New Jersey towns, it retains much of its historic atmosphere. The first homes were built about 1682, and the neighborhood was settled largely by the Dutch. It was noted for its early iron furnaces.

Below Pompton Lake the river is the Pompton River. From here on, the river becomes deeper and wider, and no difficulty will be experienced in paddling to the mouth of the stream near Singac. The river below the lake becomes more winding and is flanked by lovely homes. It is ideal for paddling and is used extensively by canoeists. Near Pompton Plains a branch which is an outlet of the famous Wanaque Reservoir enters from the right. A pleasant day on the water can be had on the stretch between Pompton and Wayne. For a longer trip one may paddle from Pompton to the end of the river, where it joins the Passaic, and then up the Passaic, if time permits, returning to take out near Singac.

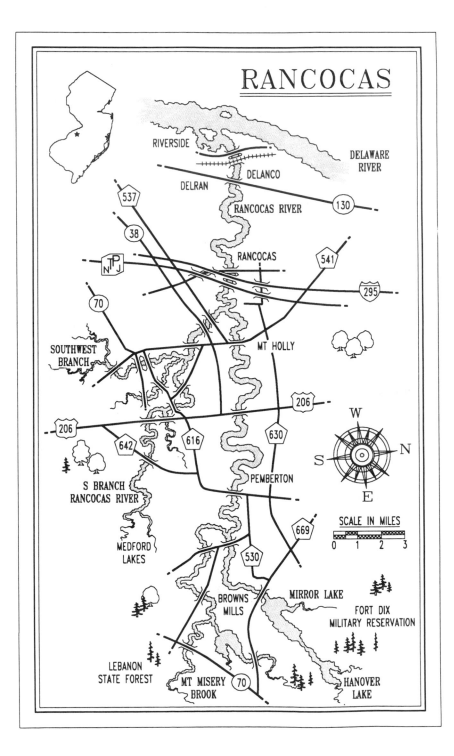

The Rancocas

The Rancocas is named for the Indians (variously called the Rancocas, Ankokas, or Ancocas) who lived along its shores. It was the highway of the tribes and the means of communication among their many villages. According to tradition their last great chief, Ramcoke, was buried in the Friends' Cemetery, near the bridge at Centerton. His was a funeral of state, and his body was borne to its resting place in a cortege consisting of a large fleet of canoes paddled by the members of his tribe.

Two small branches, together with Hanover and Mirror lakes above Browns Mills, are the sources of the Rancocas River. This section of the river—sometimes referred to as the North Branch, although it is actually the main stream—flows generally westward through the two lakes to Browns Mills. From the dam below Route 530 the river passes through New Lisbon, Pemberton, Smithville, and Mount Holly. The last few miles from Mount Holly to the Delaware River are tidewater.

The previous editions of this book have referred to and at least a generation of canoeists have known the twisting, marshy branch that enters the main stream on the left at New Lisbon as Mount Misery Creek. Mapmakers, however, call it Mount Misery Brook. It is really not much more than a large swamp brook that has its beginning in the Lebanon State Forest, with another branch north of that park near Whitesbog. The brush, growing almost down to the water, together with the swampy shores, offers few landing places for camping or picnicking. It is not pleasant canoeing water and, as a rule, is cruised only by the more adventurous who do not mind being brushwhipped, scratched by the low brush and branches, and sometimes upset.

Below Mount Holly the stream called the South Branch, which flows from another multiple-source branch, enters the main river. Its beginnings are many. One starts near the Wharton State Forest in the heart of the Pine Barrens, and another begins near Braddock's Mill Lake. A glance at a map will disclose how large a watershed the South Branch drains.

Cruising this interesting river on either the North or South Branch, or picnicking along the shores, it is not hard to visualize today the scene of two hundred years ago. It seems almost possible that an Indian birch-bark or dugout will come around the bend in the river at any time. Indian spirits seem to hover around this countryside that was once their home. But instead of birch-bark canoes, one sees today's mass-produced metal or fiberglass canoes.

The Rancocas differs in some respects from many of the South Jersey rivers, but it does have much of the lovely scenery common to those streams. On its shores are many permanent homes and

A couple enjoys the winter serenity of the Rancocas.

summer camps, but it seems wilder than it actually is and offers mile after mile of lovely natural vistas. The heavy growth of oak and other hardwoods on both shores helps create the illusion of a stream remote from civilization. The water, as is the case with other rivers that pass through the cedar swamps, is amber colored.

The motorist or hiker will find it easy to explore this stream, as main highways cross it at a dozen places between Browns Mills and Mount Holly. It is possible to drive along the river on Route 530, never more than a few hundred yards away from it, from Pemberton to the headwaters above Browns Mills. From Pemberton to Mount Holly a good road follows the south side of the stream. There are places to picnic, one being in a pine grove a hundred yards west of the bridge at New Lisbon, on the south shore. Another is the riverside park at Pemberton.

Because dams along the river keep the water deep and slow moving, there are a number of places where one can launch a canoe, paddle upstream several miles to the next dam, and then return downstream to the starting point. It is particularly delightful in the fall when the foliage is a riot of color. The Rancocas is safe for the beginner who at least knows the rudiments of canoeing, as there are few logs or other dangerous obstructions.

Canoe parties may make arrangements at Hack's Canoe Livery in Mount Holly to have their craft delivered to Browns Mills or other sites. It is a two-day journey from Browns Mills to Mount Holly.

For the lover of birds and wildlife the upper part of the stream is a delight. Deer, slow-moving blue heron, bittern, and ducks may be seen occasionally. It is said that the mockingbird sings in the neighborhood of Browns Mills in May. Holly and mistletoe are frequently seen. A series of small lakes, created by the damming of the river, makes possible many watersports and good fishing.

In the nineteenth century Browns Mills was a favorite resort spot for people of New York and Philadelphia. It is still lovely in the summer but no longer attracts summer crowds from distant cities.

For the first few miles below Browns Mills the main stream runs through such a tangle of vines and brush and twists and turns so many times that it actually bewilders canoeists who travel it. Endless beauty, with surprises around every bend, is their reward.

Wooden dam near New Lisbon Road. Dams and gates are found at several points along the Rancocas. The deep water that they provide more than compensates for the inconvenience of a portage.

In the stretch above New Lisbon the river loses some of its charm in the vicinity of a sewage treatment plant. Many canoe parties prefer to begin their trip at a convenient launch site at New Lisbon.

At Pemberton there are many interesting things to see and places to visit. Among the oldest buildings are an antique center, previously a gristmill, and at Hanover and Elizabeth streets, an apartment house, previously the ancient stage tavern where the coaches of the eighteenth century stopped. No towns are to be seen for several miles below Pemberton, until Smithville is reached.

Some twenty-five miles or more below Browns Mills is Mount Holly, where the river explorer will want to spend some time. It is an attractive community today and still retains much of the atmosphere of the past. Settled by Friends before 1700, it has developed into a typical modern and prosperous town, but its people have apparently recognized the value of its ancient landmarks.

The courthouse at Mount Holly.

This Mount Holly building is the home of America's longest-functioning volunteer fire department.

In the center of the town is the Burlington County Courthouse, erected in 1796 and regarded as one of the finest examples of early American architecture. The buttonwood trees in the yard were planted in 1805. The building is not open on weekends, but it and a number of other buildings in the old town are worth looking at from the outside.

Another Mount Holly landmark is the Mill Street Hotel, part

of which is the original Three Tuns Tavern of colonial days. It was built in 1723 and was an early stagecoach stop. Hessian troops were billeted there during the occupation by the British in 1776.

Few people of New Jersey know that the oldest continuously organized fire company in America is here. The first firehouse, a tiny building erected to house the leather buckets of the fire brigade in 1752, is now in the yard of the Relief Fire Engine Company No. 1, a direct descendant of the original fire brigade. To interested visitors the firefighters will show a small museum and the minute books, logs that provide an unbroken record from the date of the founding of the first company.

Looking downstream from Mount Holly, one sees that the river is hemmed in by high banks, heavily timbered, making the stream narrower than it is above the town. The tide comes up as far as the Mount Holly dam, and from this point to the Delaware the character of the river changes materially.

A few miles below Mount Holly the high, wooded shores give way to the lowlands, bordered for the most part with rushes and

This meeting house was built before the charming village of Rancocas grew up to surround it.

other saltwater vegetation. While it is altogether different from the freshwater reaches of the upper river, it is interesting to those who are fond of tidewater country.

Halfway between Mount Holly and the Delaware, near the right-hand shore of the river, lies the town of Rancocas. The village is not old as towns go in this part of New Jersey; few buildings date back to the beginning of the nineteenth century. However, in the surrounding countryside, there are buildings that were erected in the early years of the eighteenth century. Among them is the John Woolman plantation, the home of the famed abolitionist, whose handsome brick manor still stands. Here too stood the home of William Franklin, son of Benjamin and the last colonial governor of New Jersey. Unfortunately Franklin's home has been torn down to make way for a highway.

In Rancocas there are many lovely old brick houses, with the large chimney breasts on the end so typical of eighteenth-century buildings. In the center of the village is the Friends Meeting House, built in 1772, before the village that now surrounds it. The

Leafless trees comprise a winter scene along the banks of the Rancocas.

Ratchet lift gates controlled the water flow in the chain of lakes and the river above Mirror Lake.

people of this lovely little community are proud of their town, and once, when the New Jersey Highway Department wanted to widen the principal street through the village, the outraged residents obtained over two thousand signatures on a petition of protest and made the state officials change their minds about the necessity for the project. A bypass now serves the motorist just as well.

In the summer, the lower part of the Rancocas can become quite overcrowded with cottagers in residence, heavy weekend traffic on the many roads that cross the stream, picnickers, and the like. Pleasanter canoeing waters can be found from the source of the river at Hanover Lake through the following chain of lakes and river to Browns Mills and on to New Lisbon. Such a cruise provides plenty of paddling and comparatively quiet cruising waters.

Above Browns Mills the chain of lakes and the river connecting them are for the most part within the Fort Dix Military Reservation. Surprisingly little junk or litter spoils this area. Perhaps this is partly due to the military reservation regulations, but the cleanliness, without the usual environmental spoilage, is also due in large part to the evident pride and civic-mindedness of the people who live in the area. As we drove around an attractive, pine-covered housing area on the north shore of Mirror Lake, above Browns Mills, we came upon a Chamber of Commerce roadside sign that read:

Let no man say, and say it to your shame,
That all was beauty here until you came.

The Raritan—South Branch and North Branch

Why the early geographers chose to designate that part of the river from its source at Budd Lake to its meeting with the North Branch as the South Branch, and from that point on to Raritan Bay as the Raritan, is a mystery. Those who have explored the valleys of these streams by car or by canoe will agree that from the nature of the terrain, size, and water flow, they appear to be one river. Counting this as one stream, we have the longest river in New Jersey, over one hundred miles from its source to Raritan Bay.

The Raritan has always appealed to poets and other writers, and probably more has been written about its beauty and commercial possibilities than has appeared in print about any other waterway in the state. In 1806 John Davis, an English poet, described this lovely river in his "Ode to the Raritan, Queen of Rivers":

> All thy wat'ry face
>   Reflected with a purer grace,
> Thy many turnings through the trees,
>   Thy bitter journey to the seas,
> Thou Queen of Rivers, Raritan!

As far back as 1683 Thomas Rudyard, in his book on the American colonies, mentioned the Raritan as a river that would probably assume large importance in the commerce of the colonies. Peter Kalm, a visiting Swedish scholar, in his book of

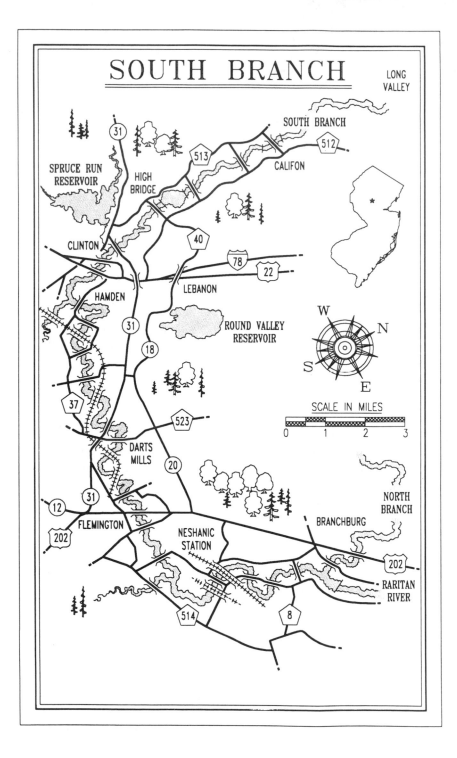

Old Queens, now the administration building of Rutgers University, was built between 1809 and 1811. A continental artillery unit commanded by Colonel Alexander Hamilton shelled the British across the Raritan River from a position near here during the retreat across New Jersey.

impressions of this country, said this river would one day be the chief water highway in America, and he also wrote at length of the beauty of the upper part of the river.

The name Raritan came from the Indian word *Laletan,* which is said to mean "forked river." Another interpretation is "smooth running" or "gentle." The villages of Naraticongs were scattered all along the shores of the river, and on it they plied their canoes from its headwaters to the bay. They used the Raritan as their chief artery of travel by canoe until the middle of the eighteenth century, and their trails followed both shores. The final act of purchase of the Indian rights and lands, before the last of the New Jersey tribes were moved to reservations, was concluded on the banks of this river.

In 1650 Cornelius van Tienhoven, secretary of the West India Company, wrote:

> The district inhabited by a nation called the Raritangs is situated on a fresh water river that flows through the center of a lowland which the Indians cultivated. This is the handsomest and pleasantest country that man can be-

Just downstream of New Brunswick, the Rutgers University boathouse sits alongside the former outlet lock where the Delaware and Raritan Canal connects with the Raritan.

hold. It furnished the Indians with an abundance of maize, beans, pumpkins and other fruits. . . . Through the valley pass large numbers of all sorts of tribes, on their way north or east. The land is, therefore, not only adapted for raising grain and rearing cattle, but also is very convenient for trade with the Indians.

The settlers who came to the valley, after van Tienhoven's report was made public in Holland, soon settled throughout the length of the Raritan. They harnessed the waters of the river to drive the wheels of countless gristmills, and although few traces of those industries remain, the original charm and peacefulness of the river are still evident.

The decline of the railroads has left many abandoned bridges along the Raritan. Near Finderne we find the unusual—a working freight line.

Low dams like this one are occasionally encountered and offer no difficulties, as the canoe can be lined over them, and in the spring the water is usually high enough to run them.

Those thrifty and hard-working Dutch built substantial fortunes from the farms and mills, and today many of their descendants are still carrying on the agricultural pursuits of their forebears, particularly in Hunterdon County. Unlike most other New Jersey counties, Hunterdon is still predominantly rural in character.

Before the surrounding lands were denuded of their heavy forests, the river was deeper than it is now. As late as 1750, large flatboats were poled upstream as far as Raritan and then floated back to the storehouses at New Brunswick with the flour and other mill products of the upper river.

The South Branch

The South Branch, particularly, still retains that aristocratic poise that gives it a character different from that of any other river in the East. Starting in the hills of Morris County as an outlet from Budd Lake, the South Branch has the character of a twisting, bubbling mountain stream as it drops over Schooley's Mountain down to Long Valley. In Bartley, at the foot of the mountain, the river turns down the valley and straightens out, taking the character of a small meadow stream. It continues through the quiet little villages of Naughright, Long Valley, and Middle Valley. After the two dams in Califon the river quickens its pace as it weaves its way through the hills to High Bridge.

The Long Valley region was heavily settled by Germans beginning in the early 1700s and was known, until World War I, as German Valley. In this area, the watchful traveler will spot the remains of several early mills along the banks of the river. Of particular note to the canoeist is the mill in Long Valley, as the mill dam is still intact and forms a rapid that should be run with caution. This is noteworthy since we have found it convenient to put in just above the mill. (From Bartley down to Long Valley, the river divides into several channels that are too shallow to canoe.) The stretch from Long Valley down to the town of Hoffmans offers a beautiful run that has frequent small rapids, but it should be attempted only by experienced canoeists. The two dams in Califon should be portaged. The five-mile stretch through the deep ravine—Lockwood Gorge—from Hoffmans to Lake Solitude above High Bridge, becomes dangerous when the water is high enough to run there, because of the huge boulders that practically fill the river (Class III–IV white water on the international scale). Even without a canoe, it is a treat to explore the first twenty miles by car and by walking along the more isolated spots.

The South Branch is a favorite stream of trout fishermen. It is kept well stocked with adult-sized trout, and good sport is the result. There is a great deal to interest the lover of scenic beauty, as well as the fisherman.

At High Bridge the river breaks through the last of the mountains, and formerly a beautiful waterfall could be seen where the seventy-five-foot-high power dam now stands. On the eastern shore, below the dam, is the Taylor Wharton Iron and Steel Company, no longer operating, but for many years the oldest continuously operated iron works in the state, and the second oldest company in North America, after the Hudson's Bay Company. Deposits of iron in the hills surrounding the town, a plentiful supply of timber for charcoal, and water power made a natural combination for the start of this industry in 1742. The beautiful stone-arch bridge just below town replaced the original wooden "high bridge" around 1865.

After breaking through the mountains at High Bridge, the river, as if to catch its breath from the tumultuous run through the rock-strewn gap, slows down to a wandering meadow stream. In all but seasons of very dry weather, those who wish to paddle a canoe on the South Branch can safely launch their boat many places between High Bridge and Clinton. There are some dams and shallows, however.

At Clinton there are two old gristmills; the one on the left bank is over two hundred years old. During the early days of this country such mills could be found every few miles on this river.

From Clinton down to Hamden the river is very attractive. Never more than a few feet deep, it twists and turns through the lovely meadowland so typical of Hunterdon County.

The South Branch from below High Bridge to Flemington Junction and beyond has become very popular with canoeing groups in recent years. It affords a delightful day of sun and recreation through the hills of Hunterdon County. Some canoeists cruise all the way to Landing Lane Bridge in New Brunswick, taking three or more days to complete the journey.

Until the Spruce Run and Round Valley Reservoirs were built and started pumping from the river, we had no difficulty with low water except during prolonged dry spells. Since pumping began, however, seeming at times almost to pump the stream dry, our canoe journeys between Hamden and Darts Mills have been more wading than paddling. With this in mind, it is generally wise to check the water level below the dam at Hamden before committing to a day on the upper Raritan.

Below Hamden the hills begin to crowd the stream again and the pace becomes a bit more hurried. On the right bank the high cliffs of traprock and shale, covered for quite a distance with a

One of the two eighteenth-century gristmills in Clinton. This one, with its operating water-wheel, now houses the Clinton Museum, which has an interesting collection of Americana.

heavy growth of spruce and hemlock, present a totally new picture. The country through here is less accessible by road and has thus retained a greater degree of wild natural beauty. Mile after mile of the same sort of scenery greets the explorer, all the way to Flemington Junction. Between Darts Mills (where the river goes below Route 523) and Flemington Junction there are three dams. The first two are often runnable, but the third requires a short portage on the left bank.

From Flemington Junction all the way to the mouth of the river the canoeing is good much of the season. There are some shallows, but not enough to interfere seriously with the cruiser. The many milldams help to back up the water in sufficient volume to enable one to cruise without too much wading. The earliest gristmills in the state were along here.

Many old New Jersey towns are passed in the journey downriver from Flemington Junction—Three Bridges, Woodfern,

Neshanic, and South Branch among them. It is easy to follow the river by car or on foot, as good roads are close to the stream all the way.

Those who have known the river for many years will recall the lovely old covered bridge that spanned the stream at South Branch. It suffered the fate of many others a few decades ago, when it was replaced by a modern concrete bridge. On the right bank of the river, just above the bridge, stood a village blacksmith shop.

The South Branch is joined by the North Branch at a place known to the Indians as Tucca-Ramma-Hacking or "the meeting place of the waters." From this point to Raritan Bay the stream is officially the Raritan River. Since the original publication of this book in 1942, the old dam just below the junction of the North and South branches has been washed out. A new dam has been built, and the old canal, extending from above the dam to the Raritan, is again filled with water.

Just below the dam at Tucca-Ramma-Hacking, on the left shore of the river, is Duke Island Park. This beautifully situated unit of the Somerset County Park System, covering an area of 250 acres between the river and the Old York Road, was the gift of Miss Doris Duke.

The nineteenth-century iron bridge over the river at Neshanic Station.

One of the many abandoned railroad bridges crossing the Raritan. This one is in Neshanic Station.

Tucca-Ramma-Hacking, the meeting place of the waters, where the North and South branches meet to form the Raritan.

Through the middle of the park runs the old canal that supplied water for the turbines that operated the original textile mills in Raritan and later provided power and light for the Duke estate, across the Raritan River. The old boating pavilion located on the canal is now an office and nature museum for the Somerset County Park System.

Duke Island Park is very popular with family groups. It has a band shell in which music events, plays, and other programs are held in the summer. Tennis, fishing, a myriad of children's play equipment, and plenty of shade for picnicking or just loafing are also major attractions of the park.

The North Branch

Unlike the South Branch, the North Branch really appears to be a branch and not a part of the Raritan River. The rugged hill country of Morris County, in which the North Branch has its

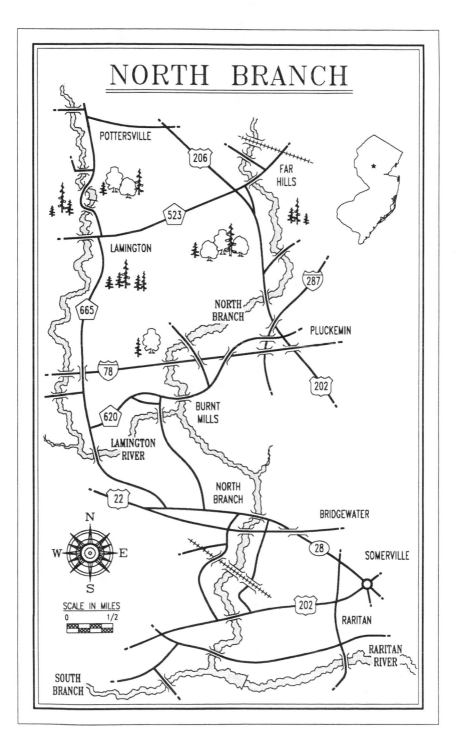

*It is early spring, and this view near the source
of the North Branch gives promise of an early
start of the canoe cruising season.*

beginning in a swamp that until a few years ago was a mill pond supplying water for the gristmill at Ralston, has more of a "sharp valley" or closed-in appearance.

This stream offers a great deal of interest for both those who may want to explore it by car and those who may want to paddle downstream. The car explorer should start at the hamlet of Ralston on Route 24 between Chester and Mendham. Here one may visit the local historical museum, which is in the building that for many years was the post office for Ralston. In fact, it was the oldest continuously operated post office in the state of New Jersey. From there follow the stream down through Peapack–Gladstone to Far Hills on Route 512. From that point continue through Bedminster on Route 202, River Road, Cowperthwaite Road, and Burnt Mills Road to the village of North Branch. The end of the North Branch is not far below.

The canoeist should begin cruising from a point about two miles south of Bedminster and plan to take out at either Burnt Mills, for a short cruise, or at the mouth of the river where it joins the South Branch to form the Raritan.

One of the oldest standing former post offices in New Jersey is on Route 24 at Ralston. Erected in 1775, the building is now the headquarters and museum of the Ralston Historical Association.

The area around Peapack and Gladstone, in the upper river valley, is of great historic interest, and on some of the surrounding hills are many elegant estates.

On the main street of Peapack may be seen the ruins of one of the earliest lime-burning kilns in New Jersey. During the late years of the eighteenth century, lime produced here was tried as an experiment on local farms to sweeten the soil and increase crop yield. The experiments were so successful that lime came into general use on farms elsewhere.

The canoeist may not wish to consider cruising the North Branch from any point above Bedminster, even during periods of high water, since the section of the North Branch that parallels Peapack Road is posted against trespass.

We class this stream as a spring cruise. Under normal water conditions the best place to start is on the west side of the Kunes Mill Road bridge, about two miles below Bedminster. During a cruise one May, however, when the water level should have normally been sufficient to paddle without too much wading, we were out of the canoe as much as in it for most of the first few miles. Cars may be left at a little dirt parking lot northwest of the

An attractive view of the North Branch from the Route 202 bridge between Far Hills and Bedminster.

An old Jersey Central railroad bridge crosses
the North Branch in Branchburg.

junction of Route 202 and River Road, just before the Route 202 bridge over the North Branch. Due to the realignment of local roads in the construction of Interstates 78 and 287, it is now difficult to follow the upper river by car.

Below the suggested starting place, the river runs straight ahead along treelined banks and under another small bridge. About a mile and a half later it passes under I–78. After that, the evidence of modern civilization is not much of an intrusion. The river continues through beautiful meadowland with the fields a riot of color created by bluebells and other spring wildflowers.

For a cruise of a half day or less, the road at Burnt Mills, just above the point where the Lamington River enters, is a good take-out place. From that point, it is only a fifteen-minute drive back to the starting place.

In the area west of Pluckemin, the absence of fences is noticeable. This is the famous fox-hunt country of Somerset County, where hunts are regularly held in season. Below the Lamington River (see "Small Streams") the water is deeper and involves less wading until the low dam above Route 22 is reached. Above the highway for nearly a mile along the river is North Branch Park, a part of the Somerset County Park System. Picnicking is permitted here, and Scout camporees are sometimes allowed, but as far as we know overnight camping is not permitted.

From Route 22 down to the mouth of the North Branch, where it joins the South Branch to form the Raritan, the water is shallow, dropping over many shale ledges and making paddling difficult.

There were once plans to place a dam near the confluence of the North and South branches, and this would have backed up the rivers for several miles as well as flooded the Old York Road toward Readington. These plans also called for water to be pumped into the North and South branches to maintain some appropriate level of water. This project, had it been approved, would have drastically changed the beautiful natural scenery of the river.

The Toms

The swampy areas through which the upper part of the Toms passes and the profusion of heavy brush on the banks of the stream make this river somewhat difficult to travel. We do not recommend it as a starter. However, the wild beauty and the clear, cold water of the river more than compensate the cruiser for the effort. The motorist will find it difficult to get more than a glimpse of the upper twenty miles of the stream. The last ten miles, where the land is more open, and the shores of the tidal estuary to Barnegat Bay may be enjoyed from a car or on foot.

Like many of the smaller, winding streams of South Jersey, this river appears to be one which should be covered by canoe in a few hours' time. The actual mileage by water from Bowman's Mill Bridge at Route 528 to Barnegat Bay is over thirty miles, however, twice the distance by road.

The network of good roads, crossing the stream many times, enables one to start a canoe trip at any one of several places, but the farther upstream one puts in, the more carryovers will be encountered. As of 1990, starting from any point above Bowman Road was doubly difficult. Not only was the summer water level low, but many trees were down. Some of the trees seemed to have been deliberately felled behind the Meadowbrook Village area.

The more temperate climate of this area in New Jersey makes it possible to travel this river in late fall, after the seasonal rains. Some parts of the stream, particularly from Whitesville, can be cruised during any season. Whatever the put-in point, we find water levels and air temperatures in May and June to be the best. October is also a delightful time to cruise this river.

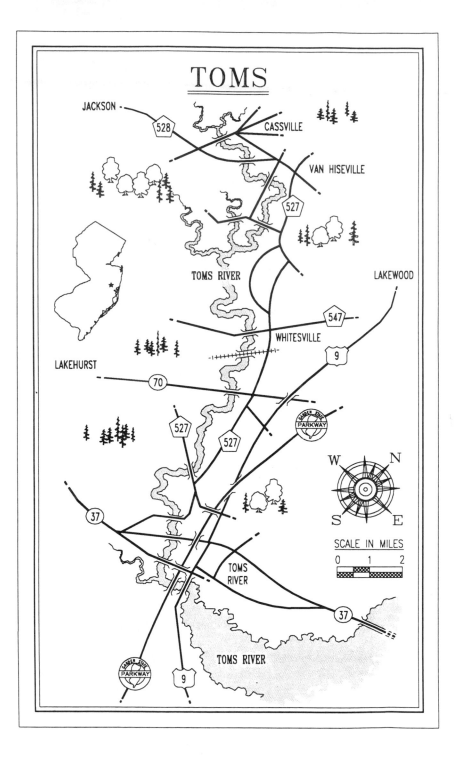

Old meets new at a Toms River lunch stop. A 1928 Old Town, built for speed, alongside a modern ABS Old Town, built for solo whitewater.

While there are the usual number of small communities along the way, none of them is large enough or close enough to the river to enable one to get meals. It is best to carry provisions with you.

The section of the Toms River between Bowman Road and Whitesville runs through typical swamp country, which becomes flooded during periods of high water in the spring. During such times the river completely loses its identity and spreads out in every direction. It is difficult to determine the main channel, and unless the tree line is carefully watched, the cruiser is likely to paddle into one of the many flooded areas without an outlet. When there is sufficient current it is possible to keep to the channel by letting the canoe drift along the faster water. Like the river above Bowman Road, this section may be in need of a river-clearing expedition before it can be said to be canoeable.

From Whitesville down to the bay, a totally different kind of country is encountered. Instead of the swampy shores found on the upper river, one will see firm, sandy soil covered with a heavy

Paint Island Spring, near the source of the Toms River, is a chalybeate spring containing a heavy concentration of supercarbonate of iron oxide in solution. The yellow solids in the bottom of the spring are commonly called ochre and were used by the Indians to paint their faces for war. This rare artifact is a paint pot, used by the Indians to hold these clays.

growth of oak and scrub pine. Through this area it is possible to go ashore and explore the surrounding country. Not so many obstructions are encountered in this part of the stream. At times the river narrows down to a width of fifteen feet, but it continues to run very fast and deep.

Below Route 70 the river opens up into a clear-running stream with mile after mile of entrancing views quickly appearing around the bends. The shores are lined with a riot of all sorts of plant life. From here to the town of Toms River it is hardly necessary to swing a paddle as the current pulls the canoe along. The Ridgeway Branch enters the river from the right at Manchester, and Wrangle Brook also joins it just above the Garden State Parkway.

A good take-out point is at Winding River Park, a beautiful strip that follows the west side of the river for about a mile north of Route 37. There are picnic facilities here, but no overnight camping.

At the bridge in the center of Toms River village, a canal-like stretch of the river is used as a mooring basin for large pleasure boats, and beyond that the tidal estuary extends seven miles to Barnegat Bay. Most voyagers on this portion of the stream end

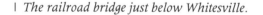

| *The railroad bridge just below Whitesville.*

Keeping one's head low is often good advice on the Toms.

Negotiating a typical pull-over tests one's balance.

| *River clearing helps everyone.*

their journeys near this bridge, as it is difficult to continue beyond this point by canoe in the tidal water.

Toms River has a colorful history dating back beyond the War of Independence. The first buildings were a blockhouse, a few houses, and a mill. In 1782 a large group of loyalists or Tories attacked the blockhouse defended by local patriots under Captain Joshua Huddy, who was forced to surrender when his supply of ammunition became exhausted. The loyalists burned the fort and all other buildings in the town and hanged the valiant Captain Huddy at Gravelly Point. This act so enraged the people of the surrounding countryside that all loyalists were forced to leave for more hospitable parts until the end of the war. Today the patriot's name graces the attractive little park surrounding the mooring basin downtown.

Members of the Murray Hill Canoe Club and the Mohawk Canoe Club have spent a great deal of time keeping the river clear of brush and fallen timber from Whitesville to Toms River. On special weekends, both clubs give power saws, brush hooks, and the like as much of a workout as paddles, instead of just enjoying cruising and camping on this interesting Pine Barrens stream.

This clearing work over the past years has made possible a three-day cruise in normal-height water from Whitesville instead of the two-day trip that was possible before the clearing projects began. It is a never-ending job, as floodwaters undercut and wash the dirt from the roots of the trees and they drop into the river.

The Wading

The Wading River, long known to experienced canoeists as one of the wildest and most beautiful of the Pine Barrens streams, has its beginnings in several small branches, both to the east and to the west of Chatsworth. On those branches are several small cranberry bogs. Because of the swamps and sometimes heavy stands of cedar, that part of the river above Speedwell on Route 563 is usually choked with fallen timber and brush, and cruising it is not practical. It calls for a lot of hard work with axe and saw.

In order to enjoy the wild beauty of this stream, it is necessary to journey down it by canoe. The traveler by car, however, may reach it at many points along the roads that run near the river or cross it frequently.

Many canoe clubs schedule cruises on the Wading every spring and fall. They keep the river below Speedwell pretty well cleared of obstacles, including the more recent beaver dams. Whenever one of the beaver dams is encountered it is easily carried around. We don't mind the little effort to negotiate them, as they seem to be a part of the wild nature of the river.

We suggest to those who may like an easy day's cruise that they launch their canoe from Route 563, four miles south of the general store in the center of Chatsworth. From that point to the best place to take the canoes out of the river again is about sixteen miles by water but only about six by road. South of Jenkins, where Route 563 again crosses the river, there is a nice shelving beach below the bridge and plenty of safe parking space off the road. To

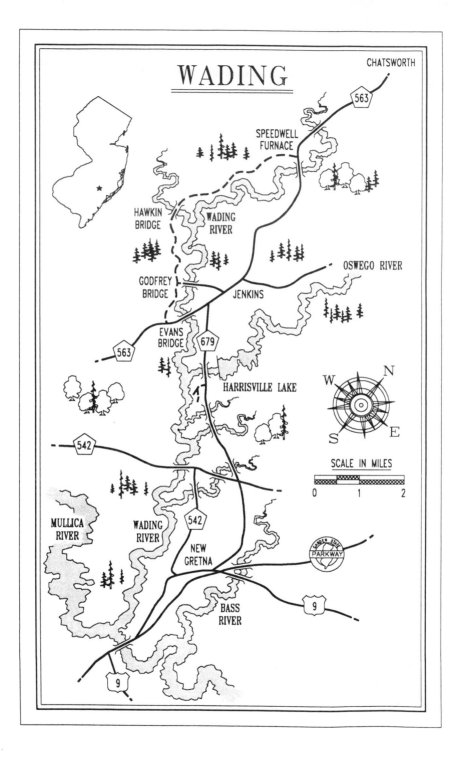

| *The river south of Speedwell Furnace.*

continue beyond this point is to battle with more open water, wind, and tide.

Those who may want transportation or to rent canoes for a cruise on this or other nearby streams will find the Bel Haven Canoe Rental to be the nearest facility. Canoe livery services can also be found on Route 563 between Speedwell and Evans Bridge. The staff can suggest the best places to start and end a canoe trip, and they know the area and conditions.

If you start your trip at Speedwell, several hours downstream you will pass the state campground at Hawkin Bridge. This is a large, primitive campground that gets a lot of use from Scout and church groups during the spring and fall. You can obtain camping permits to use this and other sites in the Wharton State Forest at the Visitor Center at Batsto. Hawkin Bridge is actually on a small stream a quarter of a mile west of the main stream. This bridge and the campground can be reached by a sand road, and it is a popular starting point for trips. A few hours farther downstream another state campground is passed. This campground is known as Godfrey Bridge and is more of a family campground. Only

Wading River along a quiet stretch.

campers staying at Godfrey Bridge are allowed to use it as a put-in or take-out point for canoes. As you pass under Godfrey Bridge you will see a large private campground on the left. This is Wading Pines Campground.

Less than an hour downstream from Godfrey Bridge and only a few minutes above Evans Bridge, where you come to the main highway, you go over an old dam or roadbed. In the spring, when the water level is high, you may pass over the dam without knowing that it is there. At other times, you can either haul the canoe over or portage on the right.

On a brilliant Saturday many years ago we decided to try a cruise from the very headwaters at a lake near Chatsworth. We had no reason to believe such a trip could be made except for general information that there appeared to be enough water to float a canoe. We reckoned without the tangle of fallen cedar trees through which we had much additional exercise in the form of axe work for the first five miles. From the start of the cruise we were surrounded with a profusion of white cedar, laurel, and other species of plants and great trees. Thousands of acres of beautiful, aromatic cedars lined the shores, with an impenetrable

| *Putting in at Speedwell Furnace Bridge.*

Hawkin Bridge, three hundred yards up the Tulpehocken Creek from the Wading River.

The landing at Bodine Field, near where the Oswego meets the Wading.

| *Chatsworth Lake.*

swampland extending for miles on both sides. It was a scene of indescribable beauty, and during the entire morning journey we did not see a single sign of civilization along the way.

Between eight o'clock and one we had progressed a distance of not more than five miles because of the difficulties of getting through the fallen timber. It seemed as if we were off in some faraway wilderness instead of within a few miles of busy state highways. And that was not the last of our adventures that day. Before we finished our trip, we enjoyed the experience of actually becoming lost, with only an hour of daylight left to find our way out to the highway. More about that later on in the story.

One of the best descriptions written about these cedar swamps may be found in *American Ornithology* by Alexander Wilson, written more than one hundred fifty years ago:

The appearance they [the white cedar trees] present to a stranger is singular—a front of tall and perfectly straight trunks, rising to a height of fifty or sixty feet, without a limb, and crowded in every direction, their tops so closely woven together as to shut out the day, spreading the gloom of a perpetual twilight below. On a nearer approach, they are found to rise out of the water, which from the impregnation of the fallen leaves and roots of the cedars, is of the color of brandy. Amidst this bottom of congregated springs, the ruins of the former forest life lie piled in every state of confusion. The roots, prostrate logs, and in many places, the water, are covered with green, mantling moss, while an undergrowth of laurel, fifteen or twenty feet high, intersects every opening so completely as to render passage through laborious and harassing beyond description; at every step, you either sink to the knees, clamber over fallen timber, squeeze yourself through between the stubborn laurels, or plunge to the middle in ponds made by the uprooting of large trees, which the green moss concealed from observation. In calm weather the silence of death reigns in these dreary regions; a few interrupted rays of light shoot across the gloom; and but for the occasional hollow screams of the herons, and the melancholy chirping of one or two species of small birds, all is silence, solitude, and desolation. When a breeze rises, at first it sighs mournfully through the tops; but as the gale increases, the tall mast-like cedars wave like fishing poles, and rubbing against each other produce a variety of singular noises that, with the help of a little imagination, resemble shrieks, groans, growling bears, wolves, and such like comfortable sounds.

The general description of the eerie qualities of the cedars and laurels still holds, but of course the giant cedars Wilson mentions have been cut during the past century and a half.

On the cruise we started out to describe, we finally managed to get to a main road by one o'clock and, since we could not find any dry land elsewhere, sat on the edge of the road to eat our lunch.

Questioning a passing native, we learned that the river was more open below us and that we would not have much trouble— except getting through a large cranberry bog a few miles below. By the time we arrived at the bog we began to worry a bit about reaching our destination before dark. Arrangements had been

*Much of the Wading above the cranberry bogs
is often blocked, and some work is required to
remove the debris.*

made to have a man drive our car to a point we had hoped to reach at the end of the day.

Our stream spread out into a wide bayou, and below was a mile-long dike. Beaching the canoe, we went up to look the bayou over, and since it was crossed with a system of irrigation ditches, we could not decide which of them would take us through the bog to the river again. We finally decided on a channel to the left of the bog and started to work our way through it. The sun was getting lower, and it appeared that we might have to spend a cold night on the river. Such an experience would not have been a new one, but it certainly would not have been comfortable in late October without blankets.

Paddling through a narrow, brush-covered opening, we found the going fairly good, only to discover, from the way the grass on the river bottom pointed, that we were paddling upstream. Retracing our route we came into what appeared to be a larger stream and soon had to carry around a big floodgate. Below the gate the river ran clear and fast, and our difficulties seemed to be over.

Rounding a bend, we swung into a large pondlike area. To our utter confusion the water then proceeded to circle the pond, and there did not seem to be any outlet. The entire shoreline failed to show any sign of the river continuing, and so we had to go back to the gate. Fifteen minutes or so of daylight remained, and we decided to leave the canoe and try to get out to a road while the light lasted. Following a narrow path, we reached a sand road and finally a main highway. A walk of two miles brought us to the river again and our car driver, who was patiently waiting.

We never did find out why we lost the river that day—whether it went underground or whether we had wandered into one of the many blind channels so common in the swamplands. The perplexing question remains as to why the river flowed so strongly to that dead end pond and point of its disappearance.

Since that first attempt to cruise the river we have run it many times but have never again got out of the main stream of the river and into the false channels, as we apparently did the first time. No one has any difficulty today in keeping to the proper channel from Speedwell downstream.

In this part of the Pine Barrens, a very interesting, centuries-old industry flourished. The art of charcoal burning had been handed down from father to son for many generations in some cases. The operator first leased pine acreage and began cutting timber with which to construct truncated cones. These were then covered with clay, and the pile was ignited. Depending upon the strength and direction of the wind, holes were poked at various places and, if the operator had practiced the art correctly, a pile of charcoal resulted after a week of burning. The operation required such careful control that it had to be watched day and night or just a pile of useless ashes would be the result of the week's work. In the days of the iron industry charcoal was used in the furnaces. According to a state forester, no charcoal burning has been done in the Barrens since 1963.

There is a fascination in the exploration of this pitch pine and cedar country that is different from any other part of the state.

This clay-covered mound with holes in it was typical of the charcoal-burning operations in the Pine Barrens. The last cone was fired in 1963.

With so much actual wilderness and so many interesting things to see, it is hard to believe the area is a part of the densely populated state of New Jersey. Good roads are plentiful everywhere, if one does not care to use the river, and many glorious hours await the motorist or canoeist. The pungent odor of the pines in the hot sun and the stronger scent of cedars will stay in your memory for days after a visit here.

Below the cedar swamps on the Wading River the country changes in character as the salt tidewater is reached. Wide areas of salt marsh are the rule, and during the fall literally thousands of ducks and geese are seen. Great areas of the lower Wading River are devoted to the cultivation of blueberries and cranberries; the crops are the mainstay of the locality.

For the uninitiated canoeist we suggest that trips on this river be planned for the early fall months, as in summer insects are abundant in the swampland. In any event the fall color makes it far more beautiful, and the crisp air makes paddling more enjoyable.

Small Streams

The rivers described in the preceding pages are the principal freshwater streams of New Jersey. On most of them it is possible to paddle a canoe for a full day or longer. There are also a great many smaller streams that may not be generally characterized as canoe-cruising waterways but are worth visiting because of the scenic country through which they flow and the important historic sites to be visited. In many places one may paddle a canoe on them for short distances, and when we explore them by car we carry a canoe along in case we may want to use it.

Our selection of the noncruising streams in the following pages may not include all those our readers may be interested in. Further exploration will reveal many others. Any state map, together with the maps at the beginning of each of the chapters on the principal rivers in this volume, will serve as guides to where to start and end a journey.

To explore any of the rivers by car, with no intention of using a canoe, little advance planning is necessary. Depending upon the time at your disposal, just decide on where you want to go, read any of the suggested literature, go to the head or mouth of the stream and follow it along.

The Black–Lamington River: Morris and Hunterdon Counties

On any nice summer day, particularly when it may be a bit warm, we suggest an afternoon of exploration of this highland stream that bears the names of two rivers but is actually one stream. Why this is so remains a mystery and known only to those individuals who mapped out the terrain years ago.

The river's source is south of Route 10, near Succasunna in Morris County. It flows through Hacklebarney State Park and below the park flows through what in New England is described as a "sharp valley" that receives direct sunlight only from midmorning to midafternoon.

The fast, shallow mountain stream, together with the shade, provides natural air conditioning for the drive along the stream to Pottersville, where the valley opens up somewhat.

For many years we fished the Black as we knew it from the park to Pottersville. Later a private fishing club closed all but a mile or so of the waters to public fishing. Today, from Rattlesnake Bridge Road (Route 665) downstream, it is stocked by the state with trout.

Below Pottersville, the Black River becomes the Lamington and is so designated to its mouth, where it empties into the North Branch of the Raritan.

The village of Lamington, down the river a bit from Pottersville, is a quiet farm community that does have some claim to fame. In the churchyard are the graves of John Honeyman, reputed to have been George Washington's spy, and his wife.

It is evident as one drives along the Lamington portion of this stream, nearly always in sight of it, that it is for most of its course a shallow, slow-moving waterway. Charming little villages, old mills, and rural scenes offer many opportunities for photography and sketching. Many canoeists believe the stream unsuitable for serious canoeing. In fact, starting a canoe trip in Pottersville is extremely difficult during most of the year, due to parking problems, private property, and low water. In periods of high water, however, the trip downstream from Pottersville is quite beautiful and gives the canoeist a different perspective of the New Jersey countryside.

Except in the dry summers, practical canoeing can begin where McCans Mills Road crosses the Lamington between the towns of Lamington and Pottersville. From here downstream, the river passes through farms, estates, and two golf courses before emptying into the North Branch of the Raritan at Burnt Mills.

An approaching spring storm on the Lamington.

The proximity of one of the golf courses prompted a harmless ruse on one club outing a few years ago. A novice canoeist was encouraged to believe that she was looking at turtle eggs beneath the water. That turtles quite commonly scatter their eggs haphazardly in the stream seemed to be an acceptable explanation for the dimpled balls she saw in such abundance passing beneath her canoe. The trick worked until a few orange "turtle eggs" were found intermingled with the rest of the clutch.

A fine take-out or launching point is where Rattlesnake Bridge Road crosses the Lamington. Ample parking is available on both sides of the road for even the biggest of expeditions. Exit 26 on I–78 is only a mile away.

From this point, the Lamington meanders a few more miles past red shale cliffs until it loses its identity among the swirls and eddies of the North Branch of the Raritan. Below this junction, the North Branch can be canoed even in the driest days of summer with only an occasional bump on the gravel of the river's bottom.

Some unusually high water on the upper Lamington during August—just enough depth for an afternoon's paddle downstream to Burnt Mills.

North Branch Park in Branchburg has excellent parking facilities and easy access to the river for those ending their trip here. (See map and details in the chapter on the Raritan.)

What we enjoy about the Lamington is its undiscovered beauty. Winter, especially with snow covering the landscape, is one of the most beautiful times to canoe this hidden gem. Happily, the discard of an irresponsible civilization has yet to mar its riverbanks, discolor its sparkling pools, or clog its pure waters.

The Cohansey River, Raceway, and Sunset Lake: Cumberland and Salem Counties

Tracing the course of the Cohansey on the map, from its source near Aldine in Salem County to its mouth where it empties into the lower Delaware River, one would believe that it offers many miles of good canoeing water. That is not the case, however, as it is not much more than a brush-choked brook, except for two small ponds and the larger Sunset Lake.

Sunset Lake, over a mile in length, was formed by damming the river above Bridgeton for power purposes. A power canal, or raceway, parallels the river on the west side through the delightful city park. Residents and particularly canoeists call the raceway "the Northwest Passage." Within the park are recreational facilities and a well-stocked zoo which attracts children, big and little. In recent years a reproduction of a Lenape village has been built in the park. There is a canoe rental house at the Franklin Drive end of the raceway. For those who may wish to enjoy a few hours of canoeing we suggest paddling through the raceway and around the perimeter of the lake.

To get to the river again it is necessary to leave the city and drive a few miles southwest to Greenwich. However, before leaving Bridgeton we suggest a visit to the county courthouse on Broad Street to see, in the lobby of that building, Bridgeton's proudest possession from its historic past. It is the New Jersey Liberty Bell, the story of which is told on the plaque on the cabinet in which it now rests:

> The bell that hangs in this belfry rang the tidings of Liberty in 1776 from the cupola of Cumberland County's first brick Court House and on every Independence Day until the Court House was razed in 1846. The bell was purchased by subscription and was cast at Bridgewater, Mass. in 1773.
>
> Tablet placed by Greenwich Tea
> Burning Chapter of the Daughters
> of the American Revolution in 1923.

Those who may be interested in further exploration of the scenes of the historic past of the region will enjoy the quiet village of Greenwich, a few miles down the river. In a fenced-off area on the main street is the Tea Burners Monument. It was erected in commemoration of the greatest event in the history of the town. Local citizens, dressed like Indians—as were the Boston patriots on a similar occasion—seized the tea stored in a nearby building and burned it on the night of November 22, 1774. Any old-time

IN HONOR OF THE
PATRIOTS OF CUMBERLAND-CO-N-J-
WHO-ON THE EVENING OF
DECEMBER 22-1774-
BURNED BRITISH TEA NEAR
THIS SITE-

The Tea Burners Monument on the common in Greenwich, New Jersey, commemorating the burning of British tea seized from a nearby storehouse in 1774.

resident of this delightful community will gladly discuss the Tea Party with anyone who may evince some interest. The building from which the tea was taken and burned is now gone, but other houses built by the earliest settlers are still standing along "Ye Greate Street," a street laid out in 1684.

From Greenwich to the Delaware River a strong tide ebbs and flows in the Cohansey. The river, like all tidal estuaries, wanders over the countryside in long loops between shores covered with marsh grass. One would not ordinarily explore this stretch of water by canoe, as there are many powerboats, strong tides, and potential sudden squalls.

Crosswicks Creek:
Monmouth and Burlington Counties

This is a small stream that wanders from its source near Woodstown through pleasant countryside much like that of some parts of the extreme South Jersey area. It can be followed by car easily and, if one is so inclined, a few miles of canoeing may be enjoyed between Ellisdale and Route 206 near Bordentown.

The origin of the name Crosswicks came from the Indian name of "Crossweeksunk," meaning "a separation."

The dam at New Egypt and the one at Woodstown were built to supply a head of water to turn the gristmill wheels. Lake Oakford, above New Egypt, is very popular for boating, skating, and other recreational activities. Below the village the creek may be followed along either shore, and it will be obvious to anyone that aside from the upstream ponds no attempt should be made to canoe the portion of the stream above Ellisdale. However, this section of Crosswicks Creek forms a fine background for an interesting historic tour of exploration.

Not far from the source of the stream is a very small settlement called Cream Ridge. There are just a few old houses along the road and, of course, an old church. The interesting thing about this quiet little hamlet is that it was here that Abraham Lincoln's father lived and worked as a blacksmith. The shop he operated has been allowed to disintegrate, and little of it is left to see. It was from here that the Lincoln family set out for the long journey to their new home in Kentucky.

Near Ellisdale is another millpond with a restored gristmill and associated buildings. Besides affording a convenient starting point for a run downstream to Crosswicks Village, this site also presents a lovely picnic spot.

Paddling anywhere on this stream, particularly in the upper portion, is best done after a day or two of rain. A rather unusual rapids may be safely run in this stretch, because it consists of hundreds of old tires! Yes, they were apparently dumped, but the beauty of the high banks and quiet, tree-canopied passages is still worth the effort.

Crosswicks, the village, requires a couple of hours to fully savor its quiet eighteenth-century atmosphere. The first point of interest is the Chesterfield Friends Meeting House, which was built in 1773. The old wagon shed and other buildings are near the meeting house on the extensive grounds. In fact, the property is so large that many people mistake the grounds for a town common or village square.

The meeting house was used as a hospital during the battle

The Chesterfield Friends Meeting House in Crosswicks.

between the Hessians and Continentals on June 23, 1778. During that engagement several cannonballs struck the building, and one of them lodged in the north wall, where it can still be seen today.

Until the early 1970s, the huge Crosswicks Oak stood on the southwest corner of the meeting house grounds. The site of a treaty between the settlers and the local Lenape Indians, it is likely that it was a mature tree when William Penn came to America in 1682.

After viewing the meeting house and grounds, walk down narrow and winding Main Street. It is still the colonial eighteenth-century village street on which many of the homes and stores are originals and not part of a restoration. The buildings are small and close to the street, and it is delightful to walk along and enjoy them.

Immediately below Crosswicks Village are the ruins of another mill of early twentieth-century vintage. Concrete foundations and millrace walls lead to a spillway or dam, which may be difficult to negotiate depending upon the accumulation of river debris. Be-

Interior of the Friends Meeting House, Crosswicks Village.

A favorite fishing spot in tidal water near the lower end of Crosswicks Creek.

yond this, the stream continues to meander toward Bordentown, becoming more and more affected by the tides in the Delaware.

Places like Crosswicks Village which remain as reminders of our earlier days are getting fewer year by year with every new superhighway. In the case of Crosswicks we hope it will forever remain as it is, which seems likely, as new and modern roads are to be found all around it, and there does not seem to be any reason for building more of them.

The Metedeconk River: Monmouth and Ocean Counties

The Metedeconk River, whose north and south branches lie between and roughly parallel to the Manasquan and the Toms, is typical of the many small streams along New Jersey's Atlantic coast.

In the first edition of this book, it was featured as a cruising river with full-chapter coverage. At that time, with a lot of cutting and removing debris from the narrow and twisting stream, we cruised it from Jackson's Mills to the bay at Laurelton. We had little

Tranquil spot along the river.

trouble negotiating the many sharp bends because we used a thirteen-foot aluminum canoe. It was doubtful even then that a much longer canoe could get through, particularly in the upper reaches.

When we again explored the stream in preparation for the second edition, conditions were such that we were doubtful about continuing to feature it as a cruising river. However, we did include it as such but warned the reader that a lot of hard work would be required to cruise it.

Today only the lower sections of the north and south branches are regularly paddled. The two branches converge just east of the Garden State Parkway a few miles above Forge Pond, named after a forge that was located on the river here in the nineteenth century. The most frequently paddled section is the south branch from Lake Shenandoah in Ocean County Park down through Forge Pond to Laurelton. This section is quite scenic and has been home to a blue heron rookery in recent years. The north branch is also scenic and is sometimes paddled from as far upstream as Brook Road, although the upper part is somewhat overgrown.

Someday, the upper sections of the river may be cleared again and the Metedeconk restored to its former status as a full-day cruising river. In the meantime, the lower section of either branch offers an enjoyable morning or afternoon paddle. While in the area, canoeists may want to visit the Jersey Paddler canoe store, located in Laurelton, less than half a mile from the river.

Stony Brook:
Hunterdon, Mercer, and Somerset Counties

On most New Jersey rivers the actual length of the stream is three to four times the distance as the crow flies. That is why Stony Brook doesn't appear to cover much of the three counties through which it flows. Nevertheless, according to the Stony Brook–Millstone Watersheds Association, this brook—and it is little more than that—officially begins near Woodsville, where three small branches meet and form the main stream. Much of the stream flows through shale cliffs and wooded countryside of suburban Princeton Township. After wandering around for some

Stony Brook at Alexander Street, a short distance above the point where the brook enters Lake Carnegie.

twenty miles, it empties into the south end of Lake Carnegie at Princeton.

For the fisherman, Stony Brook used to offer some trout fishing on a put-and-take basis. That is to say, the state put them in for opening day in April and restocked at regular intervals, and hordes of fishermen fought for elbow room in the hope of taking home a fish or two. However, as of 1990, a sign indicated that trout stocking is no longer done, at least in the Pennington area. But without the pressure of overfishing that is typical of stocked streams, perhaps a few trout might still be had.

We like Stony Brook for quite another reason: the sport of running several miles of fast water during the spring and fall freshets. Under the right conditions, it also offers a few hours' pleasant paddling under the canopy of trees upstream from Lake Carnegie on a summer afternoon.

Much of the time, especially in summer, this brook is not very deep and, under those conditions, may frankly be disappointing. For instance, following a brief but heavy overnight rain, it still appeared quite shallow as seen from several bridges, with light riffles but slow current.

On the other hand, during flood times, for those who can handle a canoe in fast and sometimes tricky water, this stream is good for a half-day trip from a start below the bridge on Route 569 to Quaker Road. Under these conditions, Stony Brook may test your skill with a single blade, and you may get wet negotiating one of the many bends. If one wants to devote a whole day to such a journey, it is possible to continue all the way through Lake Carnegie.

Planning a Trip

Planning

With the aid of this book or other books, you may plan a relaxing or challenging trip on the little rivers of New Jersey. To put in or take out of a river the maps in this book should be adequate; to explore the surrounding area, county road maps provide more detail. The U.S. Geological Survey maps give minute detail, but you will probably need several, and they are often out of date on cultural features.

First we suggest that one of our little rivers be selected. Before the actual trip, carefully explore by car that part of the stream of the intended journey, viewing the river from as many bridges and other vantage points as possible. Knowing the condition of the waters and places where a canoe may have to be carried will make a more enjoyable and easier canoe cruise. In such exploratory trips one can determine the best starting and take-out points and how to get to them. Better still, contact one of the canoe liveries listed in the back of this book for help in arranging a trip, or join a trip arranged by a local canoe club or county park system.

People at canoe liveries will be glad to suggest river routes near them. Liveries will usually deliver canoes to the put-in point and transport customers to and from their cars. They will often carry along people who have brought their own canoes if they are part of a renting party.

If you do not use the services of a livery, you will want to arrange to have a car waiting at your take-out point. If a group is going to canoe, then at least two vehicles are required to run a car shuttle between the put-in and take-out points. Typical practice

for a group is to meet at the put-in point to unload passengers and canoes. Then, with one driver per vehicle, all cars are driven to the take-out point; the drivers are brought back in a minimum number of cars. Hitchhiking back to the put-in, although still practiced by some individuals, is considered hazardous as well as unreliable.

New Jersey has a number of canoe clubs that plan group outings and offer a social setting as well as knowledge of local streams. Canoe liveries are usually well informed of clubs in their area.

There are a few locations where one can park a car, paddle upstream, and then return downstream to the put-in point, thus avoiding any car shuttle. The Rancocas River, the Delaware and Raritan Canal, and the tidewater sections of several rivers lend themselves to this arrangement. For a complete circuit that returns to the put-in without backtracking you may paddle "up" the Delaware and Raritan Canal starting at Millstone, portage to the Millstone River at a convenient point, and return down the river.

Even though the right of way on a river is for the enjoyment of all, there are many property owners who feel that the river is a part of their property, and some have posted No Trespassing signs.

A motor-camping/canoe-cruising outfit used by the Cawleys. The camp shown here was set up on the Appalachian Trail in North Carolina.

However, most property owners are cordial and ask only that canoeists respect their property, privacy, and peace, and carry away all refuse.

Finding a convenient point to launch a canoe is becoming more of a problem, as corporate property owners seek to avoid any kind of liability, and private owners consider too many visitors a nuisance. Socializing with property owners for a few moments can pave the way to continued access and provide its own rewards with stories of local history and lore.

Overnight canoe trips must be arranged with care, especially locating a spot to set up camp for the night. At most parks reservations must be made in advance and campfire permission obtained on the day of the trip.

Equipment

Before purchasing a canoe, consider checking your local library, where you may find magazines or books describing canoe

Canoes come in many flavors. Some of these are designed for cruising, others for whitewater, but all join together on this trip down the South Branch.

Carrying a canoe solo is often done of necessity, but the weight of some canoes and the risk of hitting trees make teamwork more popular.

designs, materials, and manufacturers. Local canoe retailers are listed in the telephone directory.

The first consideration is the choice of materials. Wooden, fabric, and even birch-bark canoes can be found, but aluminum, plastic, and fiberglass are more practical choices for canoeing the little rivers of New Jersey. Think ahead to the inevitable scrapes and portages. Fiberglass and plastic canoes slide over gravel, logs, and obstructions much more easily than aluminum canoes do. Canoes made of lightweight materials such as Kevlar are easier to transport and portage than those made from heavier materials; they also tend to cost more.

Canoes come in many shapes and sizes. A long canoe will generally paddle more easily than a short one of the same weight; a shorter, wider canoe will be more stable and easier to maneuver in tight places.

Paddles also come in a wide range of sizes and materials. Again, the lightweight materials are strong but more expensive. The type of paddle you need depends on the type of paddling you

A typical outfit for canoe cruising today: (left to right) lightweight paddles, waterproof clothing bags and lunch bags, the ever-present sponge, an army ammunition box, and the all-important PFD.

The proper technique for carrying three canoes is worth learning. Note the sponge protecting the paint where the bowlines cross over the hood. A good canoe rack and mastery of knots are particularly important.

do. In many of New Jersey's little rivers you will do a great deal of poling during times of low water, with corresponding wear of the tip of the paddle.

To remove water that splashes into a canoe or accumulates during a rain shower, a water scoop and sponge are handy. A scoop can be made by cutting the bottom off a plastic jug and taping the lid on. The sponge can take care of small amounts of water and leave the bottom of the canoe practically dry.

Most canoeists carry along a raincoat to discourage the rain spirits, and a change of clothes in case of an unexpected upset. Waterproof bags are useful and readily available. All loose gear should be tied in the canoe. Lines attached to the bow and stern of the canoe will help secure it for rescue or docking. Lines of this type are called painters and are typically about ten feet long.

Canoe on its side with tarpaulin rigged over it for day emergency and overnight shelter. Ample protection in any but severe storms.

Waterways, including all navigable rivers, are controlled by the U.S. Coast Guard or the Army Corps of Engineers. One U.S. Coast Guard–approved personal flotation device (PFD) per person is required in the canoe whenever it is afloat. Flotation cushions can be used to protect your knees if you paddle in a kneeling position or slide into a kneeling position for rapids.

Most cars transport canoes on a roof rack that usually attaches to the gutters. For short hauls styrofoam blocks that clip over the gunwales of the canoe can be used. These prevent damage to the roof of the car but require secure tie-downs to prevent lateral motion from wind gusts.

Camping Gear

In the past, camping and cooking gear was largely improvised, but today camping stores and catalogs offer a variety of equipment that serves the canoeist as well as the backpacker. Weight is not nearly as critical on a canoe trip as it is in backpacking, so the canoeist need not invest in the most expensive lightweight equipment.

Food

A good meal or snack can add considerable satisfaction to a day on the water or in the wilderness. Convenience packaging lets you choose drinks and snacks right from the grocer's shelf to carry on a trip. Cans, cartons, and bottles come in any size desired for drinks. Dried fruit, peanuts, and candies can be secured in press-and-seal plastic bags for easy access. Almost any trail mix will serve just as well on a canoe outing. GORP (good old raisins and peanuts) is the standard snack food.

In season, wild berries are abundant along the river courses in New Jersey. Blackberry, raspberry, and blueberry are all easy to recognize.

A canteen is a necessity on any extended trip. Water can be more satisfying than any artificial drink on a hot day. Though refrigeration is not a necessity, it is one of the more practical luxuries of our age. Today's ice chests fit easily in a canoe and can keep food fresh for more than a day.

Rubbish

Litter is fast destroying the beauty of some of New Jersey's most popular rivers. There are few trash receptacles along any river. Bring a plastic bag with you to carry out your refuse along with trash others may have abandoned.

Hazards and Safety

Canoeists face all of the typical hazards of the great outdoors plus those that are peculiar to the water environment.

Lyme disease is a seriously debilitating scourge that has hit New Jersey harder than most other states. It is carried by the deer tick, whose numbers have greatly increased in recent years. Like the more common dog tick, the deer tick embeds itself in its victim without any noticeable discomfort to the victim. As it draws blood, the tick can also transmit the bacteria of Lyme disease. The disease attacks the joints and nervous system and causes great misery to humans.

Fortunately, the ticks do not embed themselves immediately, and the best defense is a close inspection after any trip in wooded areas or high grass. However, the deer tick is much smaller and of a lighter color than the common tick, so it is difficult to spot. It is the size of a sesame seed. It does move about on its slender legs and remains visible even when the head is embedded. Of course, a doctor should be consulted if any tick is found embedded. Rocky Mountain spotted fever still remains a threat.

Poison ivy is a perennial hazard of any woodland, and river banks often seem to have a particular attraction for it. Learn to recognize the common three-leaf pattern of poison ivy and avoid it. To some people the rash is a minor annoyance that clears up in a week, but others can have a serious allergic reaction.

New Jersey, with the highest population density in the nation, has a reputation for chemical plants and hazardous wastes. Unfortunately, many of our waterways have been contaminated in the past and remain impure for drinking purposes. The condition of our rivers is improving steadily, however, and the many fish and wildlife species now seen give evidence to this. Still, it is prudent to carry along water for drinking and cooking.

Sunburn is a hazard that increases with the amount of untanned skin that is exposed. A canoeist can get "sandwiched" between bright sun from the sky and sun reflected from the water. A visored hat, long-sleeved shirt, and sunblock offer the best defense.

Surprisingly, it is still possible to get lost on some of the little rivers of New Jersey. In addition to the Great Swamp, there are several rivers that spread out in broad swampy areas. If you follow some of the smaller divergences that are tempting at times of high water, you may find yourself facing successive branchings going downstream until brush makes it impassable to a canoe. Working your way back upstream can be an ordeal. To avoid this, don't take downstream divergences unless you know they return to the river, or stick to the channel that carries the most water.

Most New Jersey rivers offer no white-water challenge. Nevertheless, they provide their most exciting moments in the spring when the water flow is high. Even a seemingly mild river can become a raging threat after heavy rains. An obstruction or snag can quickly upset a swiftly moving canoe. With a PFD it is usually no problem to get to safety.

Some hazards are predictable. A canoe that is held by a tree branch or a rock in fast-moving water is subject to forces that often defy intuition. If the canoe turns sideways, the upstream gunwale is pulled downward by the current. In this situation, many people tend to lean upstream. It is therefore not surprising that the upstream gunwale is frequently drawn underwater with predictable results. Patience, balance, and slow, careful moves can help the canoeist avoid many upsets.

Regardless of the cause of a turnover, it is worth remembering that a canoe filled with water will weigh over a ton. Stay upstream of such a missile when it is drifting free or when you are trying to dislodge it.

Do not try to stand in fast-moving water. With a PFD you can float on your back with feet pointing downstream until you reach secure footing.

Your first concern when caught with a swamped canoe is personal safety—for you and for others who may be involved. When the water is running high in the spring, it is also cold. Some canoeists revel in the challenge and wear wet suits. Most of us are well advised to get out of cold water as soon as possible. Hypothermia can sneak up quickly in moments of distraction and leave the victims too weak to help themselves.

Dams that carry only a trickle of water in summer can be tempting to run in the spring when the water is high, but they pose one of the most deceptive and lethal threats on the river. A heavy flow of water will often form a trap called a hydraulic or keeper as it plunges over a dam. Sticks or other debris can be observed moving in a continuous cycle below the dam. First they are drawn toward the dam. They are pushed deep under water as they come under the downflow from the dam, only to reappear later downstream, but not beyond the pull of the hydraulic. From there they are again drawn toward the dam to repeat the cycle. Over the years there have been a number of drownings as canoes and people were drawn back under the flow from a dam. Even rescuers have misjudged the threat and become victims themselves.

The adventurous canoeist will face a variety of new experi-

Learning basic canoeing and rescue techniques is best done under controlled conditions. Here rescue techniques are practiced in a basic Red Cross course.

ences and dangers. There is no substitute for good sense when presented with an unfamiliar situation.

An excellent way to prepare yourself for safe and enjoyable outings on the little rivers of New Jersey is to take a course in basic canoeing. The American Red Cross certifies participants in approved courses conducted each year in the state. You may contact the Red Cross or county park systems for information on such instruction.

Canoe Rental Directory

Renting a canoe can be a convenient as well as economical entry into the sport of canoeing. Most liveries will take you and your gear to an upstream put-in so you can enjoy a day cruising downstream.

It is advisable to plan ahead and to make reservations to avoid disappointment. Answers to many of the commonly asked questions about rivers served, driving directions, equipment availability, rental policies, and convenience facilities are listed in this section.

NOTE: Several companies specialize in Delaware River trips but are not listed in this book about the "little rivers." Companies that rent exclusively at lakes are not listed.

Canoe Liveries by Principal Rivers Served

Batsto

Adams Canoe Rentals, Vincentown
Bel Haven Canoe Rental, Egg Harbor
Mullica River Boat Basin, Green Bank

Cedar Creek

Art's Canoe Rentals, Bayville
Triple T Canoe Livery, Beachwood

Delaware and Raritan Canal

Bernard's Boat Rental, Kingston and Princeton
Griggstown Canoe, Griggstown

Great Egg Harbor

Lenape Park Recreation Center, May's Landing
Winding River Campgrounds, May's Landing

Manasquan

Mohawk Canoe Livery, Farmingdale

Maurice

Al & Sam's Canoe and Boat Rentals, Newfield

Metedeconk

Jersey Paddler, Brick

Millstone

Bernard's Boat Rental, Kingston and Princeton
Griggstown Canoe, Griggstown

Mullica

Adams Canoe Rentals, Vincentown
Bel Haven Canoe Rental, Egg Harbor
Forks Landing Marina, Sweetwater
Kayak King Rentals, New Gretna
Mullica River Boat Basin, Green Bank

Oswego

Bel Haven Canoe Rental, Egg Harbor
Mick's Canoe Rental, Chatsworth
Mullica River Boat Basin, Green Bank

Rancocas

Clark's Canoe Rental, Pemberton
Hack's Canoe Retreat, Mount Holly

Toms

Albocondo Camp Ground, Toms River
Pinelands Canoes, Jackson

Wading

Bel Haven Canoe Rental, Egg Harbor
Kayak King Rentals, New Gretna
Mick's Canoe Rental, Chatsworth
Mullica River Boat Basin, Green Bank
Pine Barrens Canoe Rental, Chatsworth

The following liveries allow renters to take canoes to additional locations. Check below under "policies" for details.

Al & Sam's Canoe and Boat Rentals, Newfield
Bel Haven Canoe Rental, Egg Harbor
Bernard's Boat Rental, Kingston and Princeton
Jersey Paddler, Brick
Kayak King Rentals, New Gretna
Mohawk Canoe Livery, Farmingdale
Pine Barrens Canoe Rental, Chatsworth

Adams Canoe Rentals, Inc.

694 Atsion Rd.
Vincentown, NJ 08088
(609) 268-0189

DIRECTIONS: From north: 10.3 miles south of Rt. 70/Rt. 206 circle on Rt. 206 to Atsion Lake. From south: 7.5 miles north of Hammonton
RIVERS: Batsto and Mullica
CANOES: 100 15' aluminum Grumman and Michi-Craft
POLICIES: Delivery service provided; will transport privately owned canoes; reservations advisable; reservations can be guaranteed with deposit; deposit not required
CONVENIENCES: Restrooms available; groceries—7 miles; fast food, diner—8 miles

Al & Sam's Canoe and Boat Rentals

2626 West Weymouth Rd.
Newfield, NJ 08322
(609) 692-8440

DIRECTIONS: From Rt. 40 at Malaga: 1 mile south on east side of Rt. 47
RIVER: Maurice
CANOES: 55 15' aluminum Grumman
POLICIES: Delivery service provided; will transport privately owned canoes; reservations required weekdays, advisable weekends; deposit not required; canoes may be taken within 50-mile radius of livery
CONVENIENCES: Restrooms available; groceries, fast food, diner, table service—1 mile

Albocondo Camp Ground

1480 Whitesville Rd.
Toms River, NJ 08755
(908) 349-4079

DIRECTIONS: On Rt. 571 at junction with Rt. 527
RIVER: Toms
CANOES: 8 16' aluminum
POLICIES: Rent to campers only; delivery service provided; will transport privately owned canoes; 1-day advance reservation advised; deposit required with reservation; deposit required for rental
CONVENIENCES: Restrooms available; groceries at camp store; fast food, diner, table service nearby

Art's Canoe Rentals

1052 U.S. Hwy. 9
Bayville, NJ 08721
(908) 269-1413

DIRECTIONS: Garden State Parkway to exit 80, two right turns to Rt. 9, south 6 miles on right
RIVER: Cedar Creek
CANOES: 55 15' aluminum Grumman
POLICIES: Delivery service provided; will transport privately owned canoes; advance reservations advised for weekends; deposit required with reservations; deposit required for rental
CONVENIENCES: Restrooms available; deli on premises; groceries, fast food, diners, table service nearby

Bel Haven Canoe Rental

R.D. 2, Box 107
Egg Harbor, NJ 08215
(800) 445-0953

DIRECTIONS: On Rt. 542 in Green Bank
RIVERS: Batsto, Mullica, Oswego and Wading
CANOES: 200 15' and 17' aluminum Grumman
EQUIPMENT: Backrests, center seats, waterproof boxes
POLICIES: Delivery service provided; will transport privately owned canoes; reservations advised for weekends; deposit required for group reservations; deposit not required for rental; canoes may be taken anywhere in New Jersey if returned the same day
CONVENIENCES: Restrooms available; groceries—2 blocks; table service—1 mile; fast food, diner—12 miles

Bernard's Boat Rental

Rt. 27
Kingston, NJ 08528
(609) 924-9418

Princeton Turning Basin Park
Alexander Rd.
Princeton, NJ 08540
(609) 683-5983

DIRECTIONS: To Kingston from northern New Jersey: Rt. 1 south to Raymond Rd., right onto Raymond Rd., at traffic-light intersection turn left onto Rt. 27, go through two lights, turn left before bridge. To Princeton: North or south on Rt. 1 to Alexander Rd., 1 mile on the right
RIVERS: Delaware and Raritan Canal, Lake Carnegie, and Millstone
CANOES: 50 15', 17', and 18' aluminum Grumman
EQUIPMENT: Rooftop carriers, bait and tackle, other fishing equipment
POLICIES: Delivery service provided; will transport privately owned canoes when included with group rentals; reservations advised for group rentals; advance deposit required for group reservations; deposit required for group rentals; renters may take canoes to other locations
CONVENIENCES: Restrooms available; table service nearby; groceries and deli—1 mile

Bridgeton Pleasure Boat Co.

City of Bridgeton Park
38 S. Laurel St.
Bridgeton, NJ 08302
(609) 451-8686

DIRECTIONS: Rt. 49 into Bridgeton, take Atlantic St. 2 blocks north. Or Rt. 77 into Bridgeton, take Washington St. 2 blocks west
RIVERS: Raceway and Sunset Lake
CANOES: 15' and 17' aluminum Grumman
POLICIES: Reservations not required but can be made with deposit
CONVENIENCES: Restrooms available; groceries—3 blocks; fast food, diner, table service in Bridgeton

Clark's Canoe Rental

201 Hanover St.
Pemberton, NJ 08068
(609) 894-4448

DIRECTIONS: From intersection of Rt. 38 and Rt. 206: Take Rt. 38 east 3 miles to Pemberton Borough, turn left, located on left
RIVER: Rancocas
CANOES: 50 15' and 17' Osagian and Smokecraft
POLICIES: Reservations for groups advisable
CONVENIENCES: Restrooms available: groceries—1 block; diner—3 miles; table service in Pemberton and on Rt. 38

Cranford Canoe Club

250 Springfield Ave.
Cranford, NJ 07016
(908) 709-7285

DIRECTIONS: Garden State Parkway exit 137, right from off-ramp, 1 mile to light at Springfield Ave., turn right, go two lights, on the right
RIVER: Rahway
CANOES: 29 15′ aluminum Grumman
POLICIES: No reservations; canoes may only be used locally on about 2.5 miles of the Rahway River; open Saturday and Sunday only
CONVENIENCES: Restrooms available; groceries—half mile; fast food, diners, table service in Cranford

Forks Landing Marina

Camp Swiss Ave.
Sweetwater, NJ 08037
(609) 567-8889

DIRECTIONS: From milepost 7 on Rt. 542: Continue straight onto Jackson Rd., stay on Jackson Rd. to stop sign, turn right onto Pleasant Mills Rd., 1 mile to Sweetwater firehouse, across the street
RIVER: Mullica
CANOES: 30 17′ aluminum
CONVENIENCES: Restrooms available; groceries—half mile; fast food, diner, table service in Hammonton—7 miles

Griggstown Canoe

1294 R.D. 1, Canal Rd.
Griggstown, NJ 08540
(908) 359-5970

DIRECTIONS: From Rt. 1: North on New Rd., follow to end, turn left onto Canal Rd.
RIVERS: Delaware and Raritan Canal, and Millstone
CANOES: 36 15′ and 17′ aluminum Grumman, Lowline, Mirrorcraft
EQUIPMENT: Rooftop carriers
POLICIES: Delivery service provided by appointment for groups only; reservations advised for group rentals.
CONVENIENCES: Restrooms available; groceries, fast food—4 miles; table service—6 miles

Hack's Canoe Retreat

100 Mill St.
Mount Holly, NJ 08060
(609) 267-0116

DIRECTIONS: North on Rt. 130 to Burlington, take Rt. 541 to center of

Mount Holly, turn left at fountain, one-and-a-half blocks east on Mill St. on right
RIVER: Rancocas
CANOES: 70 15' aluminum
EQUIPMENT: Rooftop carriers
POLICIES: Delivery service provided; reservations advised for large groups
CONVENIENCES: Restrooms available; groceries—1 block; fast food, diners, table service nearby

Jersey Paddler

1756 Rt. 88
Brick, NY 08724
(908) 458-5777

DIRECTIONS: Garden State Parkway to exit 91, east on Rt. 88 to the intersection with Rt. 70
RIVER: Metedeconk
CANOES: Many sizes and brands in Royalex, fiberglass, and aluminum
EQUIPMENT: Rooftop carriers
POLICIES: Delivery service provided; will transport privately owned canoes; reservations appreciated but not required; deposit required for rental; canoes may be taken by renters to other rivers
CONVENIENCES: Restrooms available; groceries—1 block; fast food, diners, table service nearby

Kayak King Rentals

P.O. Box 171
New Gretna, NJ 08224
(609) 296-8002

DIRECTIONS: Going north on Garden State Parkway, take exit 50 and follow Rt. 9 1 mile to Rt. 679, turn left onto Rt. 679 and go 3.5 miles
RIVERS: Lake Oswego, Mullica, and Wading
CANOES: Specializes in recreational (nonrolling) kayaks. Single (10'), double (13'), and sea (16–18') made by Keowee and Kiwi
POLICIES: Delivery service provided; will transport privately owned canoes and kayaks; reservations advisable; deposit required with reservation; deposit required for group rentals only; kayaks can be taken anywhere
CONVENIENCES: Restrooms available; groceries—1 block; fast food, diner, and table service within 3 miles

Lenape Park Recreation Center

P.O. Box 998
May's Landing, NJ 08330
(609) 625-1191

DIRECTIONS: Rt. 50 into Mays Landing, take 13th St. to the end

RIVER: Great Egg Harbor
CANOES: 50 15' aluminum Grumman and Michi-Craft
POLICIES: Delivery service provided; will transport privately owned canoes; reservations advisable; deposit required with reservation; deposit not required for rental
CONVENIENCES: Restrooms available; snack bar on premises; groceries, table service—half mile; fast food—1 mile

Mick's Canoe Rental

> Rt. 563, Box 45—Jenkins
> Chatsworth, NJ 08019
> (609) 726-1380

DIRECTIONS: From Rt. 72: South on Rt. 563, 12.5 miles on right at Gulf station
RIVERS: Oswego and Wading
CANOES: 225 15' and 12 17' aluminum Michi-Craft and other brands
EQUIPMENT: Backrests, ice chests, dryboxes
POLICIES: Delivery service provided; will transport privately owned canoes; reservations advisable
CONVENIENCES: Restrooms available; diner, table service nearby; groceries—1 mile

Mohawk Canoe Livery

> Squankum Yellow Brook Rd.
> Farmingdale, NJ 07727
> (908) 938-7755

DIRECTIONS: I–95 to Farmingdale exit, north on Rt. 547, first left onto Squankum Yellow Brook Rd., 1.5 miles on the left
RIVER: Manasquan
CANOES: 19 16' aluminum Michi-Craft and Grumman, 6 16' ABS Old Town
POLICIES: Delivery service provided; will transport privately owned canoes; reservations not required but deposit for reservation required; deposit for rental required only when renter takes canoe on car; canoes may be taken to other rivers
CONVENIENCES: Restrooms nearby; groceries—1 mile; diner, table service in Farmingdale

Mullica River Boat Basin

> Rt. 542, R.D. 2
> Green Bank, NJ 08215
> (609) 965-2120

DIRECTIONS: Rt. 30 to Hammonton, Rt. 542 east 9 miles, on the right (2.5 miles past Historic Batsto Village). Or Rt. 9 to New Gretna, Rt. 542 west 10 miles, on the left

RIVERS: Batsto, Mullica, Oswego and Wading
CANOES: 35 15' and 17' aluminum Michi-Craft
POLICIES: Delivery service provided; will transport privately owned canoes if with a group that is renting; reservations encouraged; deposit required with reservation; deposit required for rental
CONVENIENCES: Restrooms available; groceries—half mile; fast food, sandwich shops, pizza in Green Bank; table service nearby

Pine Barrens Canoe Rental
> Box 27, Rt. 563
> Chatsworth, NJ 08019
> (800) 732-0793

DIRECTIONS: From Rt. 72: Rt. 563 south 11 miles
RIVERS: Wading
CANOES: 135 15' aluminum Smokecraft and Michi-Craft
POLICIES: Delivery service provided; will transport privately owned canoes; reservations advisable; renters may take canoes to the Wading River, Oswego River, and to nearby lakes
CONVENIENCES: Restrooms available; groceries—11 miles; table service—7 miles

Pineland Canoes, Inc.
> R.D. 2, Box 212
> Rt. 527
> Jackson, NJ 08527
> (908) 364-0389

DIRECTIONS: On Rt. 527, 4 miles north of Rt. 70, or 7 miles south of I–95 exit 21
RIVER· Toms
CANOES: 40 15', 16', and 17' ABS Old Town and aluminum Grumman
EQUIPMENT: Rooftop carriers, seat cushions
POLICIES: Delivery service provided; will transport privately owned canoes; reservations advisable; reservations can be guaranteed with deposit; large groups must send advance deposit; deposit required for rental
CONVENIENCES: Restrooms available; groceries, pizza restaurants—1 mile; diner, table service—4 miles

Triple T Canoe Livery
> 1034 Locust Rd.
> Beachwood, NJ 08722
> (908) 349-9510

DIRECTIONS: Garden State Parkway south to exit 80, left onto Double Trouble Rd. half mile, turn right onto Locust Rd.
RIVER: Cedar Creek
CANOES: 40 15' aluminum Alumacraft and Grumman

POLICIES: Delivery service provided; reservations advised for weekends; deposit required with reservations

CONVENIENCES: Restrooms available; snacks on premises; groceries— 2 miles; fast food diners, table service nearby

Winding River Campgrounds

6752 Weymouth Rd.
Mays Landing, NJ 08330
(609) 625-3191

DIRECTIONS: From Rt. 322: south on Rt. 559 2 miles.
RIVER: Great Egg Harbor
CANOES: 32 15' aluminum Grumman and Michi-Craft
POLICIES: Delivery service provided; will transport privately owned canoes; reservations advisable; deposit required with reservations; deposit required for rental
CONVENIENCES: Restrooms available; some supplies on premises; groceries—3 miles; fast food, table service in Mays Landing

Suggested Reading

$\mathcal{E}$xploring the little rivers by canoe is quite different from an afternoon paddle or a canoe race or regatta. The streams described in the foregoing pages flow through a beautiful and historic land. To enjoy them more fully we suggest some preliminary reading about the area to be explored.

So much has been written about the Pine Barrens, the old forgotten towns and the exploits of the eighteenth-century privateers and smugglers—to mention but a few of the facets of New Jersey history—that a bit of study beforehand will quicken the anticipation. One cannot help but feel a deep sense of history on a leisurely canoe or car journey through many parts of New Jersey.

The following list of titles, though far from complete, will help inform the reader of places that will be enjoyed, depending on the degree of interest in such places. A few of the books are out of print (OP) but can be found in most public libraries. Titles available in paperback are so indicated (PB).

American Red Cross. *Canoeing and Kayaking.* Fort Wayne, Ind.: American National Red Cross, 1981 (PB).

Beck, Henry Charlton. *Forgotten Towns of Southern New Jersey.* New Brunswick, N.J.: Rutgers University Press, 1983 (PB).

————. *Jersey Genesis.* New Brunswick, N.J.: Rutgers University Press, 1983 (PB).

————. *The Jersey Midlands.* New Brunswick, N.J.: Rutgers University Press, 1984 (PB).

———— *More Forgotten Towns of Southern New Jersey.* New Brunswick, N.J.: Rutgers University Press 1984 (PB).

Boyd, Howard P. *A Field Guide to the Pine Barrens of New Jersey*. Medford, N.J.: Plexus Publishing, 1991 (PB).

Boyer, Charles S. *Early Forges and Furnaces in New Jersey*. Philadelphia: University of Pennsylvania Press, 1963.

Boy Scouts of America. Merit badge pamphlet on canoeing. Irving, Tex.: Boy Scouts of America.

Brydon, Norman F. *The Passaic River: Past, Present, Future*. New Brunswick, N.J.: Rutgers University Press, 1974.

Cawley, James S. *Historic New Jersey in Pictures*. Princeton, N.J.: Princeton University Press, 1939 (OP).

Cawley, James S., and Margaret Cawley. *Along the Delaware and Raritan Canal*. Rutherford, N.J.: Fairleigh–Dickinson University Press, 1970 (PB published by A. S. Barnes).

———. *Along the Old York Road*. New Brunswick, N.J.: Rutgers University Press, 1965.

———. *Exploring the Housatonic River and Valley*. Cranbury, N.J.: A. S. Barnes, 1978.

———. *The First New York–Philadelphia Stage Road*. Rutherford, N.J.: Fairleigh–Dickinson University Press, 1981.

———. *Tales of Old Grafton*. Cranbury, N.J.: A. S. Barnes, 1974.

Cohen, David Steven. *The Ramapo Mountain People*. New Brunswick, N.J.: Rutgers University Press, 1986 (PB).

Cunningham, John T. *This Is New Jersey*. New Brunswick, N.J.: Rutgers University Press, 1978 (PB).

Ferguson, Stuart. *Canoeing for Beginners*. New York: ARCO, 1976.

Geitler, Edward. *Garden State Canoeing*. Silver Spring, Md.: Seneca Press, 1992 (PB).

Kraft, Herbert C. *The Lenape: Archaeology, History, and Ethnography*. Newark, N.J.: New Jersey Historical Society, 1986 (PB).

Leiby, Adrian C. *The Revolutionary War in the Hackensack Valley*. New Brunswick, N.J.: Rutgers University Press, 1962.

Letcher, Gary. *Canoeing the Delaware*. New Brunswick, N.J.: Rutgers University Press, 1985.

McMahon, William H. *Pine Barrens Legends, Lore and Lies*. Wallingford, Pa.: Middle Atlantic Press, 1980.

———. *South Jersey Towns: History and Legend*. New Brunswick, N.J.: Rutgers University Press, 1973.

McPhee, John. *The Pine Barrens*. New York: Farrar, Straus & Giroux, 1968 (PB).

Menzies, Elizabeth G. C. *Millstone Valley*. New Brunswick, N.J.: Rutgers University Press, 1969.

Meyer, Joan, and Bill Meyer. *Canoe Trails of the Jersey Shore*. Ocean, N.J.: Specialty Press, 1974.

Miers, Earl Schenck. *Where the Raritan Flows*. New Brunswick, N.J.: Rutgers University Press, 1964 (PB).

Ovington, Ray, and Moraima Ovington. *Canoeing Basics for Beginners.* Harrisburg, Pa.: Stackpole Books, 1984.

Parnes, Robert. *Canoeing the Jersey Pine Barrens.* Charlotte, N.C.: East Woods Press, 1990.

Pierce, Arthur D. *Family Empire in Jersey Iron.* New Brunswick, N.J.: Rutgers University Press, 1964 (PB).

———. *Iron in the Pines.* New Brunswick, N.J.: Rutgers University Press, 1966 (PB).

———. *Smugglers' Woods.* New Brunswick, N.J.: Rutgers University Press, 1984 (PB).

Stockton, Frank R. *Stories of New Jersey.* New Brunswick, N.J.: Rutgers University Press, 1984.

van Dyke, Henry. *Days Off and Other Digressions.* New York: Scribner's, 1920.

———. *Great Short Works of Henry van Dyke.* New York: Harper & Row, 1966.

Viet, Richard F. *The Old Canals of New Jersey: A Historical Geography.* Little Falls, N.J.: New Jersey Geographical Press 1963 (OP).

Wacker, Peter O. *The Musconetcong Valley of New Jersey.* New Brunswick, N.J.: Rutgers University Press, 1968.

Westergaard, Barbara. *New Jersey: A Guide to the State.* New Brunswick, N.J.: Rutgers University Press, 1987.

Weygandt, Cornelius. *Down Jersey.* New York: Appleton–Century, 1940 (OP).

Wildes, Harry Emerson. *Twin Rivers: The Raritan and the Passaic.* New York: Rinehart, 1943 (OP).

Works Progress Administration. *The WPA Guide to 1930s New Jersey.* Compiled by the Federal Writers Project of the Works Progress Administration. New Brunswick, N.J.: Rutgers University Press, 1989 (PB).

The New Jersey Division of Parks and Forestry has published a great deal of useful and interesting information, including an official map of the state and numerous regional maps. These may be obtained at the headquarters of any of the state parks or by mail from the Department of Environmental Protection, Division of Parks and Forestry, CN 404, Trenton, NJ 08625. The following is a partial list of such materials:

The Pine Barrens of New Jersey
Map of the Pine Barrens
Stephens–Saxton State Park
Rates for Day Use and Overnight Facilities
State Forest and Park Campgrounds

Year Round Guide to New Jersey State Forests, Parks, Natural Areas and
    Historic Sites
Lebanon State Forest
Wharton State Forest
Washington Crossing State Park
Bass River and Penn State Forest
Belleplain State Forest
Canoeing in New Jersey

Many of the New Jersey county parks commissions have booklets
and maps of their parks and recreational facilities. They may be
obtained by writing to or calling the parks commission at the
county seat of the county in which you are interested.

About the Authors

There is something in the reader's encounter with James and Margaret Cawley that reminds one of the Cawleys' own encounters with old-timers along the little rivers of New Jersey. "Stop here a while, friend," they seem to say, "and we'll tell you a few things about this place." They don't, when all is said and done, tell much about themselves. Instead, they interweave strands of history, folklore, geography, and geology with narratives of river journeys remembered, observations of plant and animal life, and practical advice about canoeing.

The image one might form—of a hardy elderly couple who managed to keep their balance with one foot in the canoe and the other in the library—is an accurate one, but it is not the whole picture. Their appreciation of tranquil moments alone on the water is revealing, as is their obvious joy in recalling canoeing parties and jovial campfire scenes. Hints of a fondness for fast water, which surface here and there in comments on particular rivers, are subtle signs pointing to an aspect of the Cawley character that is all too easy for the reader to overlook.

In his eighties, James Cawley expressed a great deal of regret that the sport of windsurfing had not been developed earlier. A few snapshots will put this in perspective: Picture him at Buck Hill Falls in the 1930s, when ladies and gentlemen wore evening gowns and tuxedos to supper, hurtling down a toboggan run on skis with a pipe in his mouth—straight out onto the frozen lake, since there was no other way to stop. Picture him in the 1950s and 1960s, standing on his head on a fifteen-foot paddleboard in the middle of a lake. Picture both James and Margaret Cawley skate sailing at speeds of up to sixty miles an hour—a sport he gave up only after taking a bad fall at the age of seventy-four. Their preference in paddling, which cannot be deduced from anything within these pages, was tandem double blades. These glimpses offer a bit more insight into both the driving force and the special partnership that produced, among many other things, this book.

For James Cawley, canoeing, nature, and history were bound up together with a lifelong approach to learning that relied more on reading and exploring than on the traditional classroom experience. Education being what it was at the turn of the century, he was very lucky to have had a grade-school teacher in Bound Brook who encouraged this approach by letting him lead the class on nature walks. He began canoeing with his father, who was a member of the American Canoe Association. In 1904, at the

James Cawley at the age of twelve, in his first hand-made canoe. Peter's Brook, Somerville, New Jersey, 1904.

age of twelve, he built his own canoe, the first of many hand-made boats, out of barrel staves and salvaged boards. James joined the American Canoe Association in 1914, and a number of epic cruises—at least one of which was launched on the spur of the moment—followed in the next few years.

Between July 6 and August 3, 1915, James Cawley and a friend named Harry King canoed all the way from Bound Brook to Canada via the Raritan River, Arthur Kill, the Hudson River, the Champlain Canal, Lake George, and Lake Champlain, going on into the Richelieu River. In his log book he noted simply, "The cruise was to have ended at Plattsburgh, but since we had plenty of time, we decided to go on to Canada." Another log describes two months spent on various islands in Lake George, followed by a cruise north and then south on Lake George, Lake Champlain, and the State Barge Canal—in part, the Hudson River—ending in Albany.

For a number of years James Cawley kept his canoe, equipment, and clothes in a boathouse at Bound Brook, ready to go at any whim. He was at work in New York City on June 15, 1919, when one such whim struck. Proceeding directly to the boathouse from the train station, he started out alone on a 190-mile cruise: through the Delaware and Raritan Canal into the Lehigh Canal in Pennsylvania; fifty miles up the Lehigh to Easton; over, into, and down the Delaware to Bordentown; into the Delaware and Raritan Canal again through Trenton to Lake Carnegie; and down the Millstone from Princeton back to the boathouse in Bound Brook. He was back in the office the next week.

Not long after, this fellow met his match. She had taken the trolley to Bound Brook and paddled up the Delaware and Raritan Canal to meet some friends for a canoeing picnic at one of their favorite camping spots. "Suddenly," as Margaret described the scene for her grandchildren in 1985, "I noticed coming around a bend in the canal this canoe and paddler. It made me think of an Indian as the canoe glided along smoothly and quietly, and the paddler seemed to be part of the canoe as he exerted no effort apparently in paddling. The sky, the trees along the banks, and the water and this canoe made such a beautiful, harmonious picture that it is as clear to me today as it was on that August day in 1919."

They were married the following June. Within a decade the

Margaret and James Cawley cruising the Toms, circa 1940. (Margaret E. Cawley photo)

family had grown to include three daughters, Margaret (Peg), Jeanne, and Nancy. The family canoeing and camping trips that would remain a constant of their life together began when Peg was six months old. "I would prepare the formula and feed Peg," Margaret recalled, "while Jim carried the canoe and duffel around the locks." It could be said that this set the pattern for much of their later life.

Another constant of Cawley family life, down to this day, is music, and that seems to have been one of Margaret Cawley's special contributions. After high school she studied piano, voice, and harmony privately at the Institute of Musical Arts, Carnegie Hall, and then founded her own musical kindergarten. She was featured once as a piano soloist with the Summit Symphony Orchestra, and in her longer engagement as wife and mother, she played piano every night after putting the girls in bed. Other activities—serving as the historian of the Short Hills Chapter of the Daughters of the American Revolution, for instance—dovetailed nicely with those of her husband. Not every woman, then or now, would be at home with the idea of refinishing canoes in the dining room. It took an extraordinary amount of energy, on top of character, to keep up with the ongoing adventure while caring for an extended family of six or seven, making her own and her daughters' clothes, practicing piano, and following her other pursuits.

For nearly sixty-four years, James and Margaret Cawley were partners in marriage, camping and canoeing, historical research, photography, writing, and lecturing. A typical Friday found her preparing equipment, provisions, and children for a canoe trip that would begin the moment he arrived home. Summers in the 1930s, Margaret and the girls lived in a camp on Lake George without plumbing, electricity, or much in the way of walls, while James worked in New York or traveled the large territory in which he sold advertising for industrial publications. He would join them at the lake on weekends and for a late summer vacation. Together, James and Margaret Cawley taught first-aid and water-safety courses during World War II and served as air-raid wardens responsible for one-third of the city of Summit.

In preparing the six books they coauthored and the innumerable lectures they gave, the division of labor was roughly as follows: Whether it was a canoe cruise or a driving tour of the western states, they made the trip together. He took all of the black-and-white photographs for the books; she took thousands of color slides for their lectures. He wrote most of the text for the books; she edited his prose and checked his memory—consulting libraries and historical associations to authenticate the facts and lore he recorded. They made a remarkable team, in or out of a canoe.

The last time they paddled together was during a visit in celebration of his eightieth birthday. They were staying with daughter Nancy Jerome and her family at the Jeromes' summer cabin on a lake in New Hampshire. James was having difficulty getting around, and Margaret had heart trouble, but he insisted on what they all knew would be their farewell to canoeing. At a nearby beach, Nancy helped them into the canoe—with the stern resting on the sand—launched them after a considerable struggle, and asked them to wait there while she went home for a paddleboard.

Farther along, still cruising. (Nancy Cawley Jerome photo)

Needless to say, they didn't. By the time she got home and paddled around the bend to join them, they were out of sight. She caught up with them on the other side of the lake. And naturally, they were doing fine. They were in their element.

Cruising down the Hackensack more than half a century ago, James and Margaret Cawley stopped to talk with an elderly woman who hailed them from the bank of the river. "She told us," they wrote, "that seeing us swing by in our canoe reminded her of an earlier day"—which she proceeded to describe "with a sparkle in her eye." In reading about this encounter, it is easy to picture the Cawleys themselves in either role. The reader who swings down the little rivers of New Jersey with the Cawleys, whether in these pages alone or with a copy of this book in the dry bag or glove compartment, is rewarded with many vivid images of earlier days. And for thousands of readers, from the 1940s on, James and Margaret Cawley have earned a place in memory beside the Lenape and all of the subsequent settlers, industry builders, nature lovers, and others whose lives and stories are inextricably intertwined with these rivers.

Index